SECRET DEAL & WALMER

Gregory Holyoake
with photographs by Gregory
Holyoake & Liz Mott

AMBERLEY

This book is dedicated to Revd Stephen Edward Young, PhD, BD

First published 2021

Amberley Publishing
The Hill, Stroud
Gloucestershire, GL5 4EP

www.amberley-books.com

Copyright © Gregory Holyoake, 2021

The right of Gregory Holyoake to be identified as the
Author of this work has been asserted in accordance
with the Copyrights, Designs and Patents Act 1988.

ISBN 978 1 3981 0412 9 (print)
ISBN 978 1 3981 0413 6 (ebook)

British Library Cataloguing in Publication Data.
A catalogue record for this book is available from the
British Library.

Origination by Amberley Publishing.
Printed in Great Britain.

Contents

Introduction

Deal and Walmer, twin towns on the south-east coast of Kent, each have their own distinctive character. They enter the history books as the site of the Roman invasion of Julius Caesar in 54 BC. Kent was never again successfully invaded, not even by the powerful William of Normandy. He is dismissed in Kent as 'Duke' William – there are no inn signs here to King William I. The county retains its motto of '*Invicta*' (Unconquered).

These historic towns lie approximately 21 miles from the Continent and have been frequently targeted by invaders. Lying in the middle of this narrow part of the English Channel are the Goodwin Sands. Although this massive sandbank is a constant hazard to shipping, it acts as a breakwater when the wind is in a certain quarter and creates a safe anchorage known to mariners worldwide as the 'Downs'.

Henry VIII, fearing invasion from France and Spain, strengthened this coastline by building three revolutionary fortresses to accommodate the age of cannon warfare. In peacetime, this attracted the attention of local inhabitants who built their houses close to the seashore, thus moving from Upper to Lower Deal and Walmer, the main residential areas today.

These developing towns were visited by successive war leaders – Pitt, Nelson and Wellington. Churchill inspected this vulnerable coast when once more it became the forefront of battle during the Second World War.

Deal and Walmer began to thrive as holiday destinations during the post-war period, but then the towns were hit by immense setbacks: the decline of the extensive fishing industry, the closure of the three coal mines, and the transference of the Royal Marines to Lympstone, Devon.

Residents, however, resolutely fought a determined plan to bulldoze the former boatmen's homes and create an intrusive modern development, by creating a defined conservation area. This mile and a quarter of Georgian, Victorian and Edwardian properties have become desirable residences.

A variety of authors and artists have taken up residence in our twin towns. Thomas Hughes conceived the idea of penning *Tom Brown's Schooldays* while renting a property in Victoria Road – convenient for sea bathing. L. S. Lowry painted the panorama of *Deal Sands*, whose features include beached boats and matchstick bathers. Humorist Nat Gubbins, famous for his newspaper column 'Sitting on the Fence', kept the nation's spirits alive during the bleakest days of the Second World War. Edward Ardizzone, whose series of illustrated children's books featured the adventures of 'Little Tim', often included local landmarks. Pop star Boy George sat sulking in the family's broken van as a petulant child while his father went fishing from the pier.

The recent introduction of a fast rail service linking London and the Kent coast has provided a new invasion, this time from DFLs (Down From London) who often make Deal and Walmer their second or permanent home. Today, the area is alive with cafés, restaurants, tea rooms, bars, art and antique shops plus a weekly market. There is a revival of entertainment – theatre and music – to entertain visitors, ensuring residents adhere to Deal's motto, 'Welcome the Stranger'.

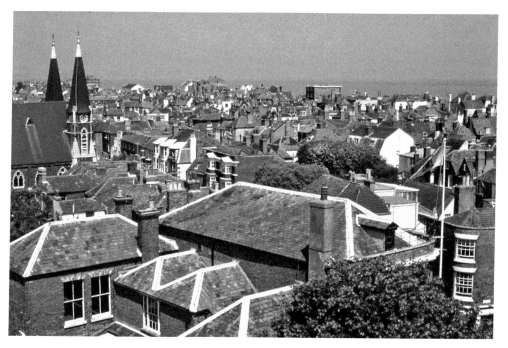

The north end of Deal from St George's Church rooftop.

1. Churches and Chapel

St Leonard's Church was originally the centre of a farming community a mile from the seashore where the town of Deal evolved over the centuries. Built on a mound – imperceptible at first – where four roads converge, it is surrounded by a host of seventeenth-century buildings. Manor House (since demolished) was built by Joshua Coppin, 'first mayor of ye corporation of Deal', at his own expense circa 1640. It boasted a magnificent carved oak staircase and a remarkable bedroom fitted up like a ship's cabin. The courthouse, opposite the church, was rented for their official meetings by the by the Borough Corporation. It retains exposed beams, pine panelling and massive fireplaces.

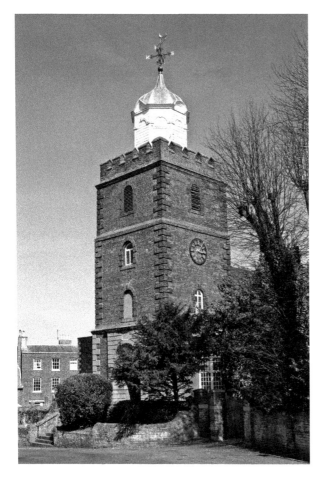

St Leonard's is the parish church of Deal.

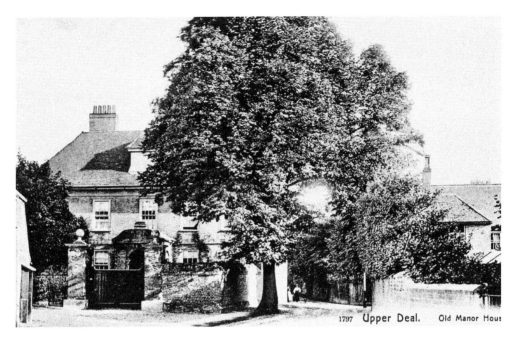

1797 Upper Deal. Old Manor Hous

The Manor House, home of Deal's first mayor.

Tormore House, formerly The Oaks, once an educational establishment for young ladies but latterly a school for young gentleman, was briefly the home of the novelist G. P. R. James. Jenkins Well is a distinctive red-brick house with twin gables and tall chimneys hidden by high walls, marking the corner site of the turnpike gate, farmed by a certain Mr Jenkins.

The Old House was formerly the Liverpool Arms, which offered sparrow shooting luncheons and bell ringers' dinners, while the Admiral Keppel (now Farriers Arms) commemorated a naval hero. Marlborough House, with its decorative shutters and shell fanlight, occupies the south-east corner of the churchyard.

The Rectory, built by Revd William Backhouse during the late eighteenth century, is a symmetrical building with an elegant porch and fanlight and a series of shuttered windows. Like the church itself, it reflects a confusing mixture of styles of architecture: a medieval cellar, a Jacobean kitchen, Georgian living rooms and a Victorian extension.

Initially, there may have been a Saxon church on this site, but the present structure has existed for 800 years. Its dedicated to St Leonard, a sixth-century French abbot who died around AD 559, the patron of outlaws and prisoners. He is often depicted girded with chains. The setting for this early church at Upper Deal was completely rural and the rector and parishioners were chastised by the bishop for grazing sheep and winnowing corn in the pleasant pastoral churchyard.

First name on the Frampton list of rectors of St Leonard's is also the most illustrious: Richard de la Wyche (1197–1253), who is commonly known as St Richard of Chichester. Richard was a farm labourer who, through his own exertions, entered Oxford University and later studied at Paris. His companion, Edmund Rich, Archbishop of Canterbury, appointed him his chancellor, but when Edmund fell from royal favour, Richard joined him in exile and was ordained abroad.

Richard returned to England after Edmund's death and was appointed rector of Deal before Archbishop Boniface called upon him to serve once more as chancellor. In 1245, he became bishop of Chichester, but shortly afterwards he died at Maison Dieu, Dover, after dedicating a wayside chapel in memory of his friend, now canonised. St Edmund's Chapel is considered to be the smallest chapel in regular use in England. It is also the only building standing dedicated to an English saint by an English saint.

St Leonard's Church possessed a tower by the twelfth century, which according to Symonson's map of Kent (1596) was surmounted by a tall steeple. During the seventeenth century the structure crashed onto the body of the church causing immeasurable damage, a not uncommon occurrence then in England. In 1686, the present replacement red-brick edifice was constructed.

DID YOU KNOW?
A striking feature of the east window of St George's Church is the lowest panel that depicts the Walmer lifeboat returning ashore, with the coastline from Deal Castle to the Timeball Tower faithfully represented.

The tower, surmounted by a white timber lantern with a cupola and weathervane, stands 125 feet above sea level. It appears on early charts of the Downs anchorage as a notable landmark for ships approaching the Goodwin Sands, and for this reason it was maintained by Trinity House. From its summit, extensive views are obtained across the English Channel towards the coast of France.

St Leonard's is entered via the tower, which contains a handsome peal of six bells, through a splendid west door, a remarkable example of Jacobean panelling. It is made without any form of brace and has a hand-wrought latch and bolt, displaying fine craftsmanship.

The interior has been altered over several centuries so that to the casual observer it presents a confusing mixture of style: a twelfth-century nave, thirteenth-century chancel, seventeenth-century tower and a nineteenth-century porch with annexe. Its present appearance is so obscure the high altar is completely hidden from view of the worshippers.

The chancel retains several important features, including an ancient aumbry (cupboard for storing sacred vessels) and a thirteenth-century double sedilia (stone seats for clergy). Prize possession is the rare Norman piscina (basin for washing vessels) mounted on an octagonal shaft.

There are seventeen hatchments (coats of arms painted on lozenge-shaped boards and placed as memorials of the deceased) representing local families: Pomeroy, Serocold, Gerard, Baker, Scriven and Harvey. The most distinguished recalls Vice Admiral Sir

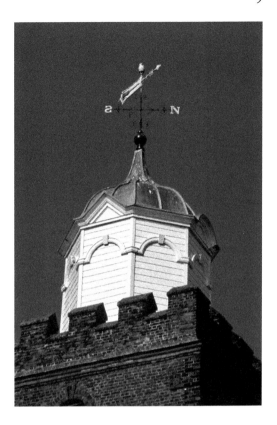

Its cupola was registered as a seamark.

Francis Samuel Drake (died 1789), a descendant of the Elizabethan seafarer Sir Francis Drake. His hatchment bears the familiar Drake crest – the world surmounted by a ship.

Three notable memorial brasses appear. On the east wall of the chapel appears a handsome brass to Thomas Boys (died 1562) gentleman-at-arms to Henry VIII at the Siege of Boulogne. He was made mayor of Calais and later the second Captain of Deal Castle under Edward VI. A second brass recalls Thomas Baker (died 1508) appointed deputy by the mayor of Sandwich to represent him at Deal when it was still a mere limb of that prominent Cinque Port. Baker, ominously, is depicted with a purse for collecting fees for neighbouring Sandwich, although charitably he left money for the repair of St Leonard's decaying steeple. A third example is a rare chrism brass, that of a newly baptised baby, in memory of an infant (died 1606) buried by broken-hearted parents under the high altar. The child is shown wrapped in swaddling clothes with a Latin inscription, composed by her father, the rector.

Over the centuries the original horsebox pews have been replaced and three galleries added, one of which presents the royal arms of William III. King William signed Deal's charter, converting it into 'a Borough and Market Town', no longer a limb of Sandwich. Joshua Coppin, newly elected mayor, ordered this to be displayed prominently in the church porch.

The tiny gallery over the west door was constructed by the pilots of Deal after the steeple crashed and destroyed their own exclusive gallery in 1658. Two small panels, difficult

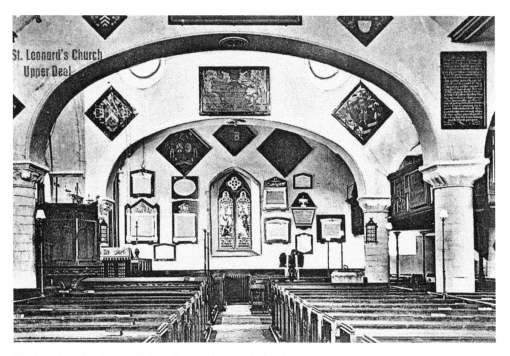

The interior of St Leonard's is replete with historic hatchments.

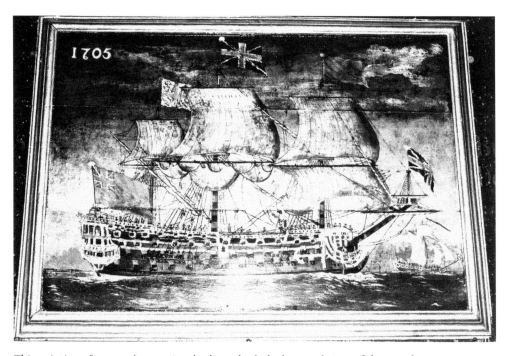

This painting of a man-o'-war uniquely shows both the bow and stern of the vessel.

to decipher, depict pilots in Restoration costume holding sounding lines. A magnificent painting at the centre depicts a three-masted man-o'-war, fully rigged and flying the red ensign. It commemorates the Great Storm of 1703, when thirteen ships of Queen Anne's navy were wrecked on Goodwin Sands with loss of 1,100 seamen's lives. Deftly, the artist has included both the bow and the stern of this noble vessel.

DID YOU KNOW?
A strangers' burial ground, where the bodies of unknown drowned seamen thrown up on the foreshore were buried, had been in use since the mid-seventeenth century. The site is now occupied by a row of modern homes.

The rapidly expanding population of Lower Deal, which arose to serve shipping becalmed in the Downs anchorage, created a necessity for a place of worship to be built closer to the seashore. Clearly, it had become an inconvenience for sailors to walk to St Leonard's Church, particularly when stationed for a few hours only in the port while awaiting a favourable wind to carry their ship on a worldwide voyage.

Chief advocate of a new church was a former mayor, Thomas Powell, who, despite opposition, organised a subscription list to affray costs, supported by the Admiralty, and building began in earnest. Champion of the cause was Admiral Sir Cloudesley Shovell, whose fleet was frequently anchored in the Downs. Shovell was the finest seaman of the age – his reputation was only eclipsed by Nelson. Alas, he was shipwrecked off the Scilly Isles in 1707 owing to imprecise navigation, and interest by the Royal Navy in this laudable project waned.

For ten years four walls were left open to the sky – 'an object of pity waiting for a roof'. Eventually, an Act of Parliament authorised a tax to be levied on coals entering the Port of Deal for twenty years. The mayor and Corporation mortgaged the coal dues and construction was completed so that in 1716 Dr Wake, Archbishop of Canterbury, consecrated the new chapel of ease, dedicated to St George the Martyr. It remains a handsome Queen Anne structure to grace Deal's High Street.

Light, spacious, dignified ... the chapel was hailed as 'a decided ornament to the town'. Galleries were added on three sides, including one on the north side for the mayor and Corporation. A top gallery on the west side was exclusively for seamen, who were provided with their own staircase so they would not interrupt the service by the sound of their heavy boots as they left abruptly when their ship was about to depart. The roof, regarded as a masterpiece of construction, is held by a massive unsupported 80-foot beam and it is surmounted by a cupola. Originally, there was a three-decker pulpit and high horsebox pews, but the cumbersome mayor's chair (1759) has been preserved.

An early perpetual curate, Dr Nicholas Cater, dominated the congregation as incumbent for fifty-six years. On the east wall is a memorial tablet recalling his favourite daughter, Mrs Elizabeth Carter, who resided at Carter House in South Street. Mrs Carter was

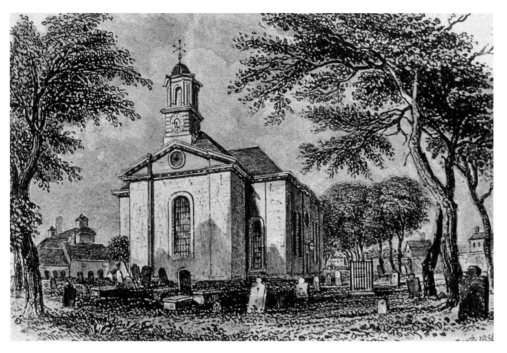

A Victorian engraving of St George's Church.

a Georgian bluestocking, an erudite scholar who spoke nine languages and composed an Arabic dictionary. When she translated the works of a first-century Greek scholar, Epictetus, she achieved fame worldwide.

The chancel contains a unique tablet in memory of the loyal service of a sailor, Commander David Ross, erected by William IV, 'The Sailor King'. Friendship arose between Ross, a midshipman, and Prince William, then Duke of Clarence, when they served together aboard Admiral Hood's flagship, HMS *Barfleur*.

When St George's was elevated to a parish church in 1852, its first vicar was Henry Honywood D'Ombrain. A parson with a passion for roses, D'Ombrain introduced the Maréchal Niel (yellow previously had proved an elusive colour) and Bourbon roses. He founded both the Royal Horticultural Society and the Rose Society, and contributed articles on gardening under the pseudonym 'D. Deal'.

The churchyard contains numerous tombstones recalling coastguards, pilots, pursers, shipmasters, captains' clerks, officers of the East India Company and the Navy Yard. Memorials of naval engagements of the Napoleonic Wars are located in the south-west corner. The square monument honours Captain Edward Thornbridge Parker, Nelson's close companion, killed in the daring midnight raid on the French flotilla off Boulogne – Nelson's only defeat. Nelson attended his funeral and stood weeping leaning against a tree, which, alas, can no longer be identified.

Originally, St George's was approached via a semicircular recessed low wall with a wrought-iron gate and lanterns. The church itself stood above ground level and was originally entered via stone steps through the present north and south doorways. Before

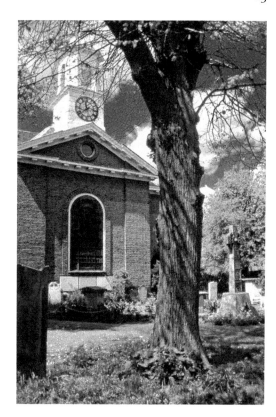

St George's Church remains a decided
ornament to Deal's High Street.

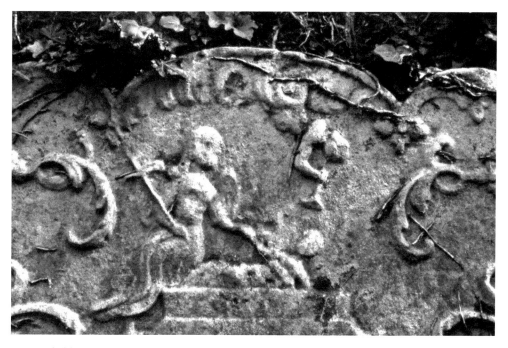

A remarkable gravestone featuring the raising of the dead.

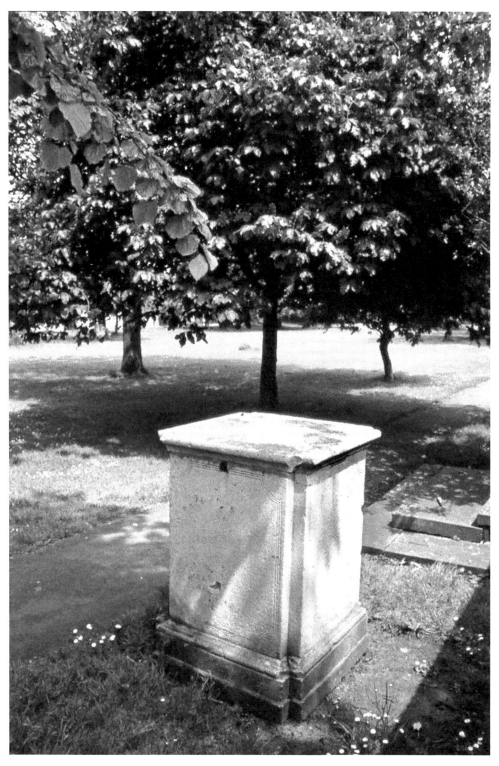

The tomb of Nelson's companion, Captain Edward Thornbridge Parker.

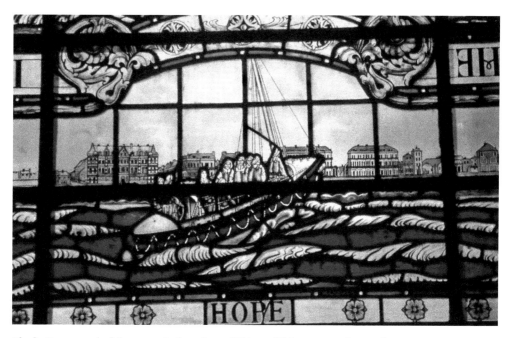

The bottom panel of the east window shows Walmer lifeboat returning to shore.

the church stands a Celtic cross and a war memorial, whose roll of honour includes the names of two brilliant sons of Revd William St Clair Tisdall. Sub-lieutenant Arthur St Clair Tisdall, a prodigious scholar who held a double first in classics, was killed at Gallipoli and posthumously awarded the Victoria Cross.

DID YOU KNOW?
When a modern church was constructed at Mill Hill to serve the mining community of Deal in 1934 St Richard was chosen as its patron.

2. Tudor Castles

Three castles that keep the Downs – Deal, Walmer and Sandown – were built by Henry VIII in 1539/40. After his quarrel with the pope over his intended divorce of Catherine of Aragon and his assumption of head of the Church in England, the king feared invasion from Catholic France or Spain and proceeded to strengthen the Kent coastline. In addition, the building of these three fortresses, a mile apart, coincided with Henry's controversial decision to publish the 'Great Bible' in English.

These revolutionary fortifications built for the age of gunpowder represent the final stage of castle architecture. Accidentally reflecting the emblem of the Tudor rose, their design consists of a round keep surrounded by a double circle of 'petals' or bastions. Deal – the 'Greate Castle' – is sexfoil while Walmer and Sandown, flanking it, are quatrefoil. Low, squat and concealed from enemy shipping, their circular construction was not only intended to deflect enemy cannonballs but would provide a complete 360-degree field of gunfire.

Traditional medieval features were retained by the architect, Stephan von Haschenperg: a central well, a dry moat, a drawbridge on the landward side and a gatehouse protected by a stout, studded door with 1,100 iron bolts and a wicket door and portcullis. Overhead are five 'murder holes', intended for pouring boiling oil on the heads of invaders.

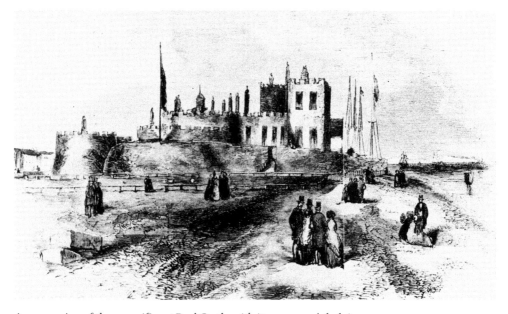

An engraving of the magnificent Deal Castle with its governor's lodgings.

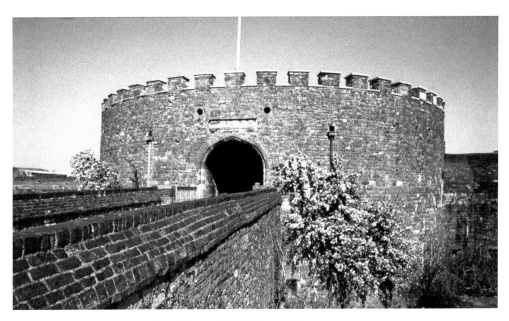

The fortified entrance to Deal Castle is on the landward side.

The trio of castles were constructed in record time – eighteen months – but work was disrupted by the earliest strike on record. Workmen downed tools and demanded a pay rise from 5 to 6 pence daily. Five of the ringleaders were imprisoned in Canterbury and four at Sandwich Gaol.

Eventually, Deal Castle's complement of 'great gunnys' consisted of one cannon, three culverins, four demi-culverins, five sacres, two minions and one falcon. The brass canon's bore was 7 inches and its extreme range was over 3 miles, while the lesser guns, such as the falcon, carried smaller shot further but did less damage. There was a short delay in firing this new weaponry for want of an 'ingineer'.

Deal Castle was so far advanced by the winter of 1539 that it welcomed a royal visitor. Henry's fourth prospective bride, Anne of Cleves, crossed over from the Lower Rhine to Calais (then English territory) shortly after Christmas Day. She was escorted across the English Channel, having never before seen the sea, by a grand flotilla under the command of the Earl of Southampton. After landing safely at Deal this demure German princess 'tarried there a certeine space in a castell newlie built' before proceeding in driving rain to meet her royal husband near London.

Ironically, none of the three Henrican castles saw hot fighting until the English Civil War (1642–51) when they passed repeatedly between Parliament and Royalist hands. Initially, they were held firmly by Parliamentarians but the declaration by Oliver Cromwell that Christmas should be celebrated by fasting resulted in a Kentish rebellion.

Sandown Castle is notorious for the imprisonment of the regicide Colonel John Hutchinson. He was one of the judges who condemned Charles I to be executed after the bitter conflicts – King vs Parliament – of the English Civil War. His name appears as one of the signatories (third in the third column) of the death warrant for the embattled king.

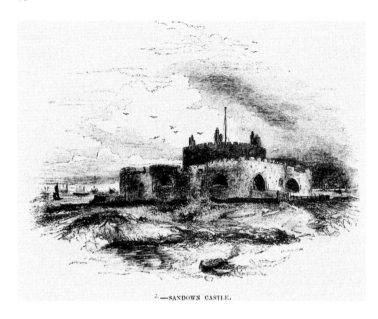

—SANDOWN CASTLE.

Magnificent Sandown Castle before it was encompassed by the sea.

DID YOU KNOW?
Chalk and flint for the construction of the three castles were quarried at nearby Mongeham. Disgruntled workmen breaking their backs in providing building materials for the defence of the realm against Roman Catholic invasion from the Continent jested they were digging the 'Pope's Hole'.

After the Restoration of the Monarchy, Charles II was swift to bring retribution upon the regicides responsible for the death of his father. Hutchinson escaped the dire penalty of being hanged, drawn and quartered but was, instead, imprisoned in the Tower of London where its governor treated him with severity. In May 1664, he was transferred to Sandown Castle, travelling under armed escort by boat to Gravesend and then on horseback to Deal.

In her biography of her husband (published posthumously) Lucy Hutchinson described his arrival at the derelict castle:

> ...a lamentable old ruined place, allmost a mile distant from the towne, the roomes all out of repair, not weather-free, no kind of accommodation either for lodging or diet, nor any conveniency of life. Before he came, there was not above halfe a douzen souldiers in it, and a poore Lieftenant with his wife and children and two or three Cannoneers, and a few Guns allmost dismounted, upon rotten carriages.

Shortly afterwards, Lucy followed her husband to the coast. Denied accommodation at the castle, she took lodgings with her son and daughter in the 'cut-throat towne of Deal'. From there they walked daily to dinner and back after the lieutenant's wife agreed to board the colonel at an exorbitant rate. Meanwhile, for diversion, he was allowed to walk under escort along the shore, collect seashells and sketch them back in his gloomy cell.

The colonel's end was inevitable. He contracted pneumonia and suffered, despite medical attention from an army doctor, a lingering death on 11 September 1664. Captain Samuel Tavernor, who was present at the colonel's demise, divined through astrology that Lucy's husband had been poisoned.

Lucy Hutchinson further rehearses a ghost story. The following spring 'there came an apparition of a gentlewomen in mourning ... and affrighted the guards mightily at first, but after while grew familiar to them, and was often seene walking in the Colonell's chamber and on the platforme, and came sometimes into the guard among them.'

Sandown Castle succumbed to the inundation of the sea and was demolished at the end of the nineteenth century. Stone from the ruins was spirited away for private or public use and turned up in the most unlikely places: the Wesleyan Chapel, Boatmen's Rooms and the abutment to the Victorian pier. Recently, the derelict site has been transformed into a tranquil and colourful community garden by a team of volunteers to add pleasure to a leisurely stroll northwards along Deal's seaside promenade.

Since the eighteenth century Walmer Castle has been the official home of the Lords Warden of the Cinque Ports. After the Norman Conquest five south-east coastal towns – Sandwich, Dover, Hythe, New Romney and (in Sussex) Hastings – were formed into the Cinque Ports, charged with protecting the coastline from invasion. Rye and Winchelsea were incorporated as 'Ancient Towns', and Deal was affiliated as a 'limb' of Sandwich.

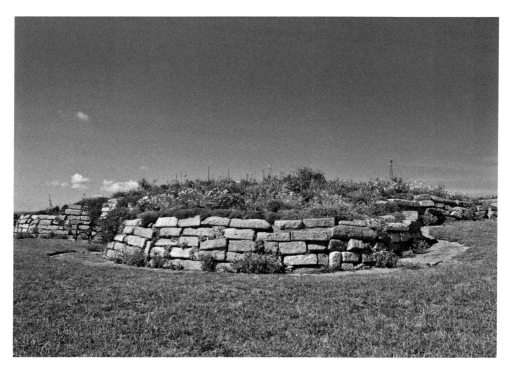

A community garden has been created around its original stonework.

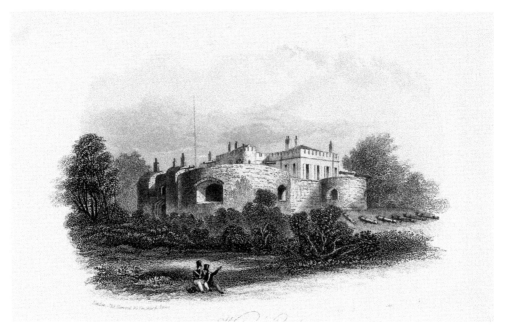

Walmer Castle is the official home of the Lord Warden of the Cinque Ports.

The Lord Warden, who held considerable powers, was responsible for regulating the affairs of the Cinque Ports. Early resident Lord Wardens were Lionel Sackville, 1st Duke of Dorset; Robert D'Arcy, Earl of Holdernesse; and Frederick, Lord North, 2nd Earl of Guilford.

Britain's youngest prime minister, William Pitt, was personally appointed Lord Warden by George III in 1792. Billy Pitt was at the time chronically in debt, which was ironic since he was previously in charge of the nation's finances as Chancellor of the Exchequer.

He had plenty of money at his disposal now to convert Walmer Castle from military to domestic purposes. He created a spacious drawing-cum-dining room on the seaward side, although the food still arrived via a circuitous route and was invariably cold. Among his surviving furniture is a gaming or library chair where the occupant sat astride in reverse position, his arms on padded rests, to study a book propped on a tiny lectern at the back.

Pitt was a generous and welcoming host. His grand supper parties gave him opportunities to sport the uniform of Lord Warden: blue jacket with red collar and facings. He joined his guests (they included William Wilberforce, champion of the abolition of slavery) partridge shooting, riding with hounds and hunting basketed hares. He rented a cottage for younger members at the entrance to the castle grounds, now known as Liverpool House.

He expanded his territory. He created a path along the beach before the castle to assist the Preventive Men in pursuit of smugglers. He extended the meadows northwards and acquired a farm adjacent to the castle where he reared fine horses and fat hogs. He soon earned his reputation as 'a gentleman farmer'.

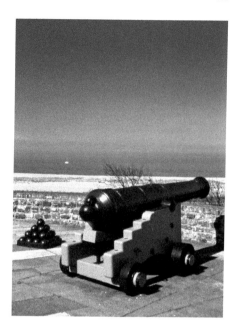

A cannon guards the castle ramparts.

Britain's arch enemy, Napoleon Bonaparte, who rose swiftly from First Consul to Emperor of France, attempted to dominate the English Channel. Pitt immersed himself manfully in the protection of the nation. He raised the militia, regular army and Cinque Port Fencibles (consisting of both infantry and cavalry) where he proudly rode ahead as their colonel commandant.

He built Walmer Barracks to house infantry and cavalry plus a naval hospital in 1795 and a shutter telegraph system linking the Downs anchorage with London's Admiralty in 1796. Further afield Martello towers and the Royal Military Canal were constructed in Sussex.

DID YOU KNOW?
Deal Castle is strangely positioned. Apart from the north-west bastion, it lies entirely in the parish of Walmer.

Pitt's solitary life at Walmer Castle was transformed by the arrival of his eccentric niece, Lady Hester Stanhope, in 1803. She took over the role of hostess for her uncle's guests, acted as his nurse whenever he was ill with gout and claimed wildly she acted as his deputy in military matters during his absence. Realising his passion for horticulture, she enlisted soldiers from Dover Castle to create a woodland garden in the deep quarry beyond the paddock. This has been restored by English Heritage to allow visitors access to her picturesque plantation, the Glen.

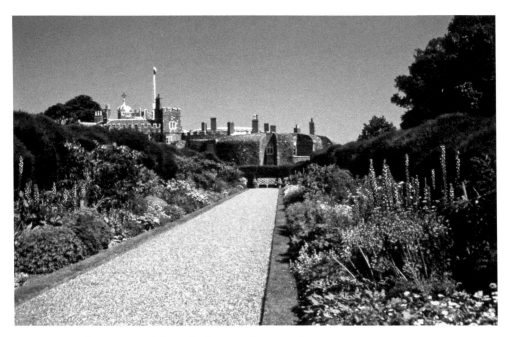

The Broad Walk with its undulating hedge at Walmer Castle.

A most illustrious Lord Warden was Arthur Wellesley, 1st Duke of Wellington, who finally defeated Napoleon at the Battle of Waterloo. Installed in 1829, he was so delighted by his 'charming marine residence' that he returned his salary into public funds. The Iron Duke resided at the castle every autumn for almost a quarter of a century.

His neighbourliness is legendary: he bathed from the beach at Walmer, he attended balls at Deal's Assembly Rooms and he went on shopping sprees to Dover. He was glimpsed hurtling down country lanes driving a succession of carriages, pausing only to offer a military salute to passers-by.

The highlight of his residency was a royal visit from the young Queen Victoria and Prince Albert in the autumn of 1842. Their Majestys enjoyed an unofficial seaside holiday and strolled, unrecognised, with their dogs on the beach towards Kingsdown. The queen caught a cold and the royal visit was extended, but upon leaving she declared the castle the most uncomfortable of all her residences.

Every Sunday while in residence the duke rode over to the Norman church of Old St Mary's, a great Bible tucked under his arm, where he tied his horse to the ancient yew tree nearest the porch. He would curl up in one corner of his private pew under the triple-decker pulpit and fall asleep during the long sermon, snoring loudly. His square pew on the north side has long since disappeared, but the duke's hatchment, showing only his Order of the Garter, is displayed.

The duke's study/bedroom in the south-west bastion is preserved exactly as he knew it, with the great mahogany desk in the window recess where he stood to write his correspondence, the wing armchair in which he died in 1852 and the narrow camp bed that accompanied him on his campaigns. When Lady Salisbury asked how he could sleep

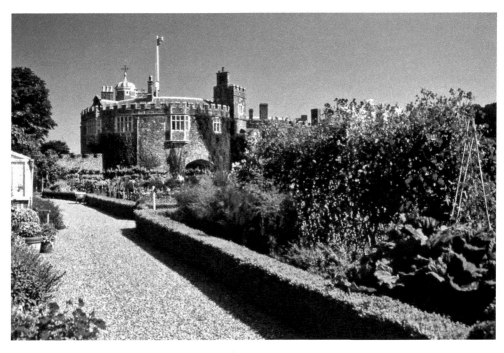

The colourful kitchen garden at Walmer Castle.

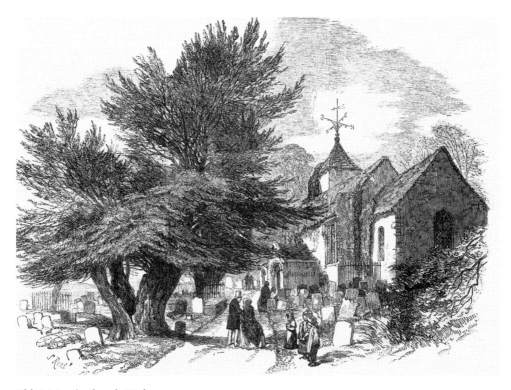

Old St Mary's Church, Walmer.

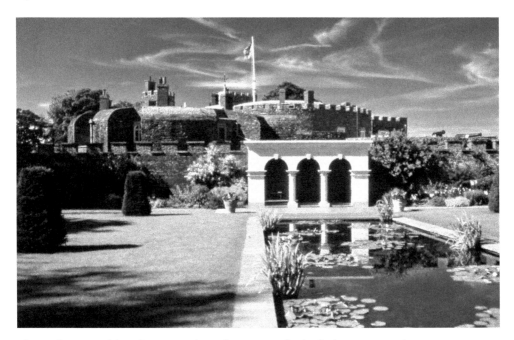

The garden created for a former Lord Warden, Queen Elizabeth, the Queen Mother.

in a bed where there was little room to turn, his classic response was: 'When it's time to turn over, it's time to turn out!'

More recent Lords Warden number Sir Winston Churchill, Sir Robert Menzies, Prime Minister of Australia, and the first female appointment, Queen Elizabeth, the Queen Mother, for whom Penelope Hobhouse converted the kitchen allotments into a walled landscaped garden. The present Lord Warden is First Sea Lord, Admiral of the Fleet, Baron Michael Boyce.

DID YOU KNOW?
Last time Deal Castle was defended against invasion was during the Second World War. A direct hit by a German bomb demolished the hideous Governor's Lodging. Local inhabitants considered Hitler had done Deal a favour!

3. Boatmen and Their Craft

Deal and Walmer boatmen were famous throughout the world for their skill and daring. Their formidable tasks were accomplished in the most tempestuous seas and their compassion in saving lives earned them high regard. Before being superseded by steam, their noble craft made a stupendous sight – with their protruding bowsprits, masts, capstans and tackle – when beached in an almost continuous line from Sandown Castle to Kingsdown Cliffs.

But were these boatmen saints or sinners? In 1867, a Lloyd's correspondent proclaimed they were a reckless force that charged an exorbitant rate for their maritime services. George Byng Gattie, in his *Memorials of the Goodwin Sands* (1890), expressed an opposite view and affirmed they were 'honest and respectable'. Nevertheless, the boatmen were often accused of 'wrecking' and were even referred to as 'Deal sharks'.

Local boatmen made a precarious living from supplying anchors and chains to homeward-bound ships that had slipped their cables in adverse weather, and for taking fresh water, provisions, men, letters and newspapers to outward bound ships in the Downs anchorage. These activities all came under the curious term of 'hovelling', which

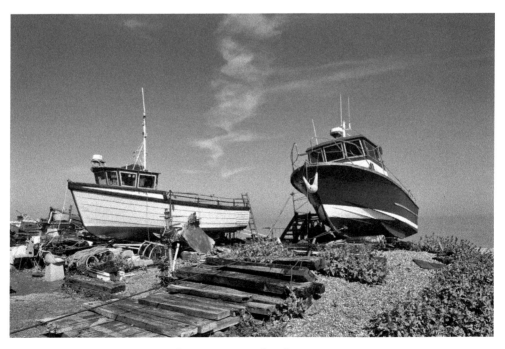

A medley of boats, winches and lobster pots on Deal seafront.

may have derived from 'hobilers' (light cavalry charged with guarding the coast against invasion during the Middle Ages).

A hoveller ('huv'ler') was also employed in 'sweeping' the seabed with grappling irons for lost anchors, cables and ordnance – dangerous obstacles to shipping. This proved a hazardous task, since boats became overloaded by the weight of retrieved artefacts, yet the work was lucrative. Recovered items were sold in anchor fields adjacent to Deal Castle and South Sandy Lane (Blenheim Road).

There was fierce rivalry between local boatmen who worked on the four distinct stations – Deal North End, Deal South End, Walmer Road and Kingsdown – that sometimes escalated into open hostility. At the first hint of a vessel in distress the boatmen swiftly launched, cutting across the bows of rival boats and sailing close on their windward side, in order to be first to put a man on board. They were expert at recognising the nationality of every anchored vessel by the way she carried her masts and arranged her yards so that they might calculate the amount they could charge for their services.

Deal and Walmer boatmen, whose knowledge of home waters was unrivalled, also offered their services as unofficial pilots in the English Channel. They would race out immediately upon sighting a ship's signal, burning blue lights, firing rockets or flying the ensign upside down, in order to be first to secure the commission to guide a vessel out to sea or into the Downs. Boarding a vessel in rough weather was a perilous mission and serious accidents occurred. Captains in full sail or steam refused to slow down – speed was essential – so that prospective pilots were forced to clamber aboard while their ship was in tremendous motion.

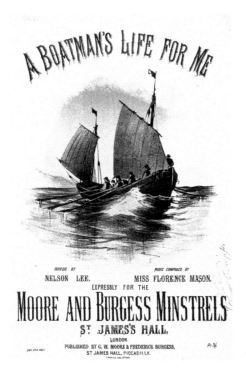

'A Boatman's Life For Me', Victorian song sheet.

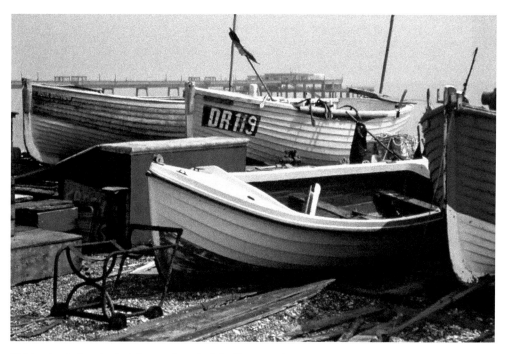

Fishing boats beached at the south end of the Promenade.

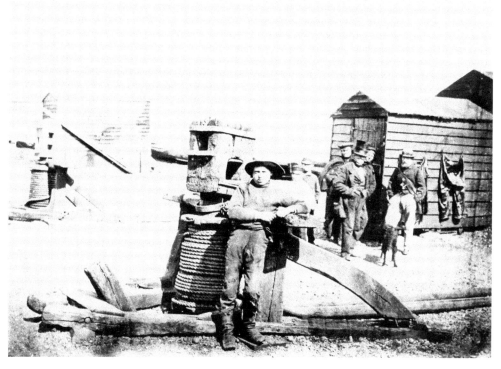

An idle moment, leaning against a wooden capstan.

Luggers, which were the working boats of Deal and Walmer, were the most famous beach craft worldwide. They were the largest class of boat that could be launched or beached from our steep, shingle shore safely in heavy seas. They were clinker built of English elm and ballasted with bags of shingle. Crucially, they were long, lean, open boats with a shallow draught, allowing them to reach areas of the Goodwin Sands where rival craft dared not venture.

They were sailed but could also be rowed. They were from 40 to 50 feet long with a 12- or 13-foot beam. In winter they were equipped with two masts: the foremast carried an enormous square dipping lug sail often with a topsail, while the mizzen, positioned well aft, had a standing lug, but there was also a storm jib set out on a long bowsprit. Their summer rig, however, involved fitting a third mast amidships equipped with another lug sail that would send the craft ahead of the fastest ships that sailed alongside them.

Luggers were also called 'forepeakers' because of a small cabin forward of the main mast. This cabin, known as a 'cuddy' or 'caboose', was furnished with bunks, lockers and a stove. There, a crew of a dozen men lived in cramped confinement in all weathers for upwards of one week. At times crews would be involved in 'West'ard cruises' when they

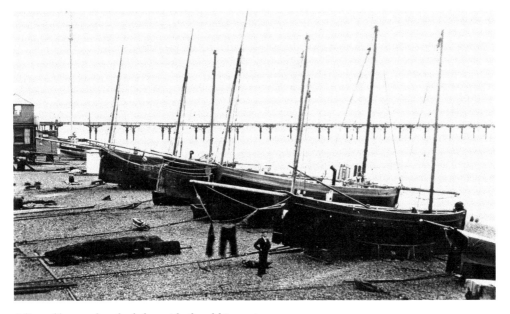

A line of luggers beached alongside the old iron pier.

would sail down Channel to meet homeward-bound ships at The Start. Sometimes they went as far as the Scilly or Channel Islands.

Although there is little recorded about the early luggers, several of the later ones achieved fame. The South End lugger *England's Glory*, manned by a superb crew, was invariably the first boat to arrive at a salvage operation. *Tiger*, an immense lugger employed specifically for ferrying the heaviest anchors and chains, was owned by a team of shareholders. *Diana*, a noble lugger, named after an earlier boat, became notorious after being apprehended carrying a staggering amount of contraband.

The dedication of skippers sailing as far as the Isle of Wight searching for ships requiring a pilot often resulted in tragedy. *Pride of the Sea* was destroyed on the rocks of Shanklin Bay in 1887, while *Walmer Castle* was lost off Ventnor in 1892. *Reform*, one of the most heroic luggers, was involved in a tragedy closer to home when she launched in a gale in January 1871. Almost immediately she became entangled in the Victorian iron pier where she was smashed to pieces and almost all her crew were drowned. The mayor headed a funeral procession attended by 300 boatmen through the streets to St Leonard's Church.

The last lugger left on Deal foreshore was *Cosmopolite*, which was displayed as a curiosity until, exposed to the elements, her timbers finally rotted and she was broken up for firewood just after the First World War. Her stern outrigger, mizzen mast and long bowsprit were ingloriously improvised for washing line posts in gardens of Lower Walmer.

Galleys that were rowed but could also be sailed were normally 28 feet long with a 5-foot beam. Galleys, also known as 'long eights', carried a single mast with a dipping lug sail but no jib. They were banked for between four, six or eight long oars, known as 'sweeps'. Unusually, they were launched stern first and therefore they had either a transom or beaching lute stern. These long, light, graceful boats possessed an amazing turn of speed and on calm days could easily outstrip every other type of boat in the water.

Galleys rowing more than four oars were illegal since they could serve no other purpose than smuggling. Invariably, they were painted white to merge with the surf so that they

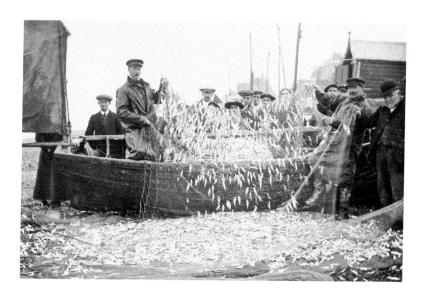

A good haul of sprats!

were screened from pursuers. Smuggling galleys might be 40 feet long and carried an enormous press of sail. They were flat bottomed and constructed with hollow beams so that they could conceal a variety of contraband, from snuff to silk. These admirable craft could be pulled across to France in under 3 hours and, laden with contraband, they could be dragged over the Goodwins, rowed across the Downs and landed in Deal or Walmer before the fast revenue cutter, in hot pursuit, could sail round the Sands.

After the Second World War only four galleys remained. Thomas Upton's eight-oared galley *Seaman's Hope* and Flint Robert's *Our Boys* were presented to the Rowing Club in 1937. Two further galleys are exhibited at Deal's Maritime and Local History Museum: *Saxon King*, a four-oared galley built in 1892, and *Undaunted*, the last seaworthy galley on Deal beach.

Boatmen's working clothes may have been a survival of the uniform of Deal's Navy Yard. Crews of local boats spent hours working in driving spray and their apparel kept them warm even when soaking wet. Men wore oilskins, consisting of trousers – 'fear-noughts' – that reached up to their armpits, plus long coats fastened with ropes that covered their knees. Top clothes were heavy cloth jackets, buttoned closely over their blue woollen jerseys, and painted overalls with pumps or thick leather Wellington boots. Long woollen scarves or 'mufflers' were wound tightly round their neck, but sou'westers – 'dread-noughts' – worn in foul weather might be exchanged for woollen or sealskin caps in summer. Boatmen wore bowlers as they turned the wooden capstans to haul luggers up the steep beach, but they exchanged them for derbies when the men strolled to church on Sundays.

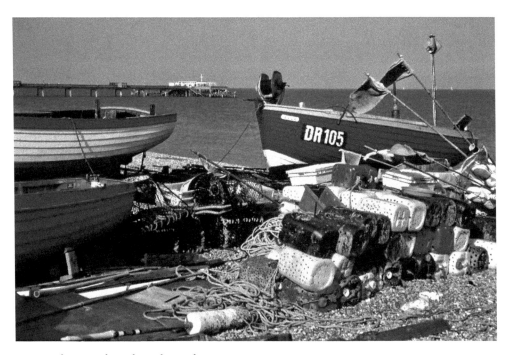

Boats and nets with Deal Pier beyond.

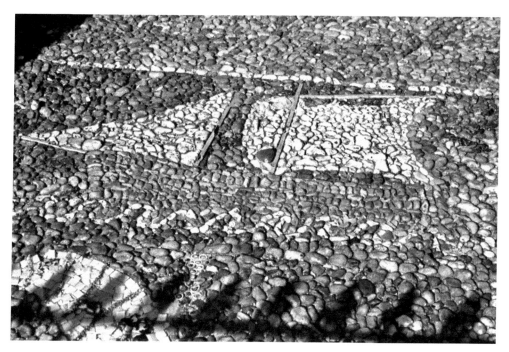

An example of the boatmen's artistic skills.

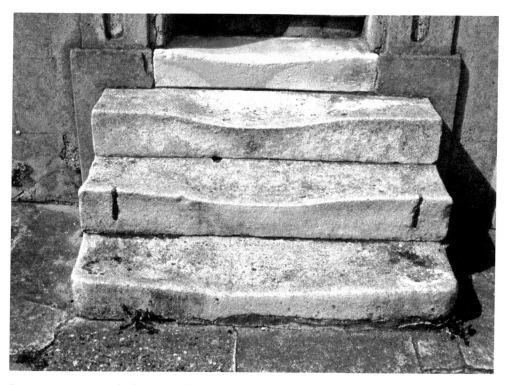

Doorsteps worn away by boatmen's heavy sea boots.

Deal provided the best boatbuilders in the world. Their handicraft was the product of generations of practical experience and might be commissioned from as far away as Australia. Premier boatbuilder was Thomas Hayward whose workshop was at the end of Cottage Row (Wellington Road). The Hayward family – father, son and grandson – produced a number of admirable luggers – *Dart, Renown, Forester's Pride* – during the nineteenth century. Their trade card presented a variety of their handicraft: a yacht, a lugger, a galley punt, a whaler and a ten-oared galley (an illegal vessel since it would only be employed by smugglers).

Each summer between the wars luggers were fitted out with gaff sails as pleasure boats. They made a glorious sight when launching – all sails set – directly off the open beach, overloaded with passengers, tightly packed on their plank seats, for a trip round the Goodwins. Tripping motorboats – *Skylark, Titlark, Moss Rose, Britannic, Lady Beaty* and *Lady Haig* – were confined to the South End. These craft were clinker built and highly varnished with either counter or elliptical sterns. They made an impressive appearance with their polished brass fittings and stern staff flying the pilot flag or the red ensign. Boatmen stood on the Promenade wearing peaked 'cheesecutters' with white tops, white shirts and navy blue guernseys, calling out 'half an hour trips', 'just a-going out' and 'lovely on the water'.

Boating parties were arranged each summer for visiting anglers who relished the prospect of fishing with rod and line around the sunken wrecks of the Goodwins. They were served by a fleet of motorboats launched stern first with reverse gear that enabled them to pull away easily from the shore. Modern craft numbered 'Dido' Redsull's *Lady Violet*, Joe Mercer's *Sidney* and *Olive*, and 'Jumbo' Bett's and Freddie Upton's motorised foresail and mizzen punts, respectively named *Terrier* and *Fishermen's Pride*. Beached along Central Parade were the fleet owned by Tommy and Hannah Upton – their boathouse was replete with flower baskets and swearing parrot – consisting of the galley punt *Skipjack*, the elliptical sterned *Margaret*, and the powered mizzen punts *Ida* and *Minnie Ha-Ha*.

At the commencement of the Second World War, sturdier motorboats were removed from the beach, which was heavily defended, but gaps were left for smaller craft to launch during the fishing season. During the evacuation of Dunkirk in 1940, every available motorboat along the south-east coast was requisitioned by the Royal Navy. Their crews, formed from mariners or landsmen, raced across to France where they repeatedly ferried allied troops to their transport ships in deep water while constantly under heavy fire from enemy fighter planes. Ten fishing boats left from Deal and Walmer, including *Gipsy King, Lady Haig, Rose Marie, Britannic* and *Golden Spray II*. Walmer lifeboat, crewed by members of the Royal Navy, was also commandeered for Dunkirk, but she sustained

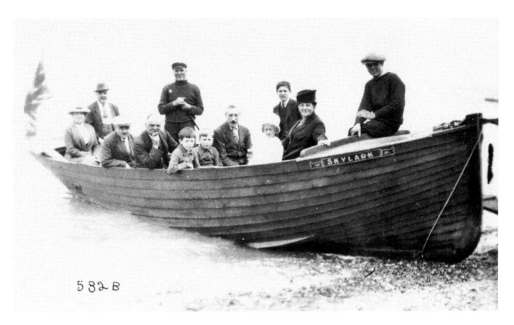

All aboard the *Skylark*.

considerable damage. A wartime edition of *East Kent Mercury* paid tribute to the gallant efforts of local boats in evacuating the British Expeditionary Force.

DID YOU KNOW?
Our oldest remaining boat, *Lady Irene*, is beached, restored, opposite Deal Castle. During autumn and winter she was employed for herring and sprat fishing while in summer months she became a tripping boat. She has acquired an engine plus a high counter stern for a smooth launch backwards into the waves.

4. Smuggling

Deal, situated so close to the Continent, was the epicentre of smuggling in England. A long, lonely shingle beach upon which small craft might glide at night, undetected by the revenue men – what more might a smuggler require? Local boats, guided by flashes from flink pistols, signal fires and hooded lanterns, slipped silently onto the foreshore on misty, moonless nights. Once landed, contraband was spirited away on loaded wagons through the narrow streets of North Deal to remote inns such as the Jolly Sailor and Noah's Ark, or large warehouses on the exposed neighbouring Sandhills.

Almost everyone in the town was involved in the 'midnight trade' – the boatmen who were the actual carriers, landlords of public houses who recruited them, and magistrates who financed their nefarious activities. Deal acquired the dubious but undisputed reputation of being the most notorious smuggling town in the whole kingdom.

Customs officials were initially concerned with collecting duties on the export of raw wool, which was discouraged in order to foster the manufacture of woollen garments in this country. English raw wool was regarded as the finest in the world and it was greatly desired by skilled weavers on the Continent. Free traders who dealt in wool were termed

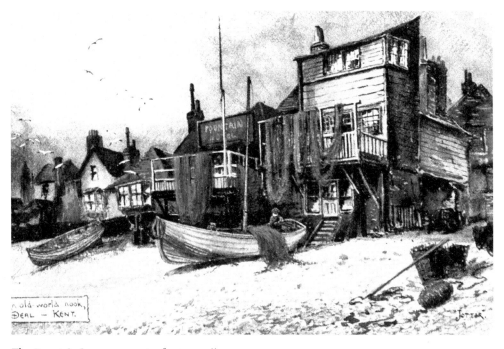

The Fountain Inn was a centre for smuggling.

'owlers' since they smuggled by owl light, and their activities were concentrated mainly in the grazing pastures of Romney Marsh.

The earliest recorded incident of smuggling in this area concerns wool. One February night in 1617, the owlers were busily engaged in transporting fifteen packets of raw wool from Sandwich to the coast to be loaded onto a Dutch vessel anchored in the Downs. Two law abiding citizens raised the alarm – a rare instance. The owlers were arrested and their goods confined in a storehouse in Deal. Alas, the Lord Warden's officer, John Clark, in charge of the storehouse, was in the pay of the Dutchmen and connived at the owlers' escape.

DID YOU KNOW?
The tombstone of Private John Elbeck of the Westmoreland Regiment, shot dead while assisting customs officers (25 September 1794), is displayed at Deal Maritime and Local History Museum.

For centuries wool smuggling was the main concern of smugglers locally, but inevitably 'run' goods turned to luxury items as duties were imposed by the Treasury to pay for a succession of wars. High taxation made smuggling lucrative and the Kent owlers turned their attention from wool to spirits, tobacco and tea (introduced into England in the mid-seventeenth century by the East India Company).

The heyday of smuggling was from the mid-seventeenth century to the early nineteenth century, when the expansion of world trade was coupled with the need for financing wars with both France and America. Concurrent with the beginning of the Dutch Wars in 1688, when taxation rocketed, was the invention of the fast, sleek yacht that assisted customs officials in their pursuit of Kent boatmen as they transported illicit cargoes across the Channel.

The commencement of the American War of Independence in 1775, however, meant that England was bereft of fighting men who were drafted abroad. This opened up further opportunities for smuggling gangs to operate along the south coast. During the Napoleonic Wars the importation of French goods was prohibited while at the same time revenue cutters were requisitioned for the war effort.

Taxation escalated as wars intensified. Duties were extended to wines (French, Spanish and Portuguese) and materials (Lyons silk, Chantilly or Valenciennes lace). James I abhorred smoking, which gave rise to the heavy taxation of tobacco. After the Restoration of the Monarchy in 1660, there was a tremendous trade in tea between China and Europe and it remained expensive until the tax was slashed by William Pitt in 1784. Curiously, the prime minister replaced it with a universally hated window tax.

Upon the accession of George III in 1740 there were 800 items on which duty needed to be paid, yet over the next fifty years hundreds more goods became liable for taxation. Alcohol that attracted high duties included brandy, rum, whisky, port wine, cordials and

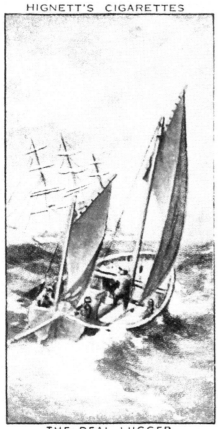

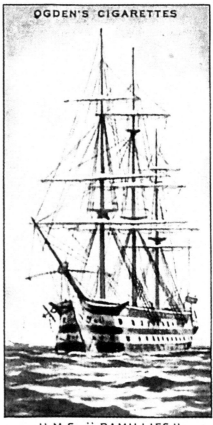

Above left: A Deal smuggling lugger shown on a cigarette card.

Above right: The revenue cutter HMS *Ramillies* on a cigarette card.

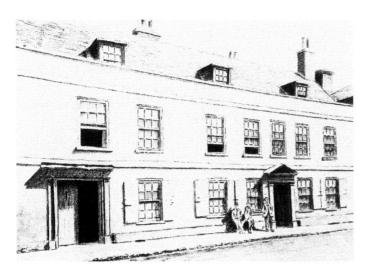

The old customs house stood in Deal High Street.

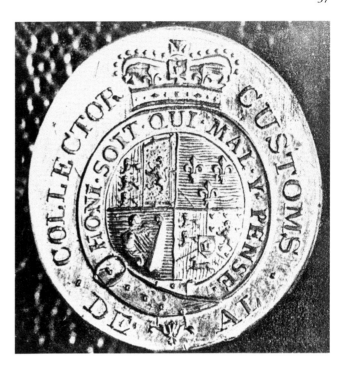

Deal customs house seal.

Dutch Geneva (gin). Luxuries taxed – and consequently ripe for smuggling – numbered coffee, chocolate, cocoa, ivory, perfume, gold rings, pearls, damask, velvet, calico, cambric, satin tiffany, gold and silver brocade.

Contraband followed high fashion, particularly among gentlewomen, who sported their purchases of fine attire at balls, dances and supper parties. Illicit items included ribbons, laces, shawls, caps, lappets, shoes, leather gloves, silk slippers, bead purses, lace handkerchiefs and ostrich plumes for their elaborate hats. As such, smuggling became romanticised.

Oddities smuggled were starch, soap, straw, salt, pepper, vinegar, paper, dice, wire, dried fruits, hair powder, scented snuff, sealing wax, coffin nails, currants, counterpanes and coconuts. At the height of the French Wars there was a specialised trade in spies, newspapers and despatches.

During the Napoleonic Wars there was a specialised trade in smuggling gold coins across the English Channel. After the French Revolution the country's currency collapsed and the price of gold soared through devaluation at the height of hostilities with England. The French Empire remained solvent by purchasing English guineas, minted from pure gold and worth 30 shillings abroad. It was estimated that gold, valued at £10,000, was smuggled out of this country every single week.

English guineas were conveyed to Paris under military escort and from thence to Spain to pay troops engaged in battle against Wellington during the Peninsular Wars. Napoleon, who opened the ports to Kent smugglers, boasted that at his final conflict of Waterloo most of his finances were raised in London. Deal smugglers who exported gold, clearly, were not inhibited by feelings of patriotism.

Death galleys were ingeniously constructed to provide an express service for 'guinea runs'. Cheaply constructed, they were 60 feet long, carried two small auxiliary lug sails and bore maximum keel. They were exceedingly fast yet perilous to handle. They lacked cargo space since gold coins were secured in leather purses strapped around the oarsmen's waist. Death galleys were expendable. They were required for a single trip only: a night-time dash across the English Channel.

The death penalty was imposed upon convicted smugglers but rarely carried out, and only then if the offender was guilty of either murder or violently resisting arrest. After execution, the bodies of criminals were ordered to be cut down and 'anatomified'. Milder deterrents were impressment into the army or navy and transportation to America or Australia.

DID YOU KNOW?
Smuggled brandy was easy to detect by customs officers since it was imported clear. Caramel, which gave it a distinctive honeyed tincture, was added only after duty had been paid.

Deal smugglers, however, did not hesitate to baulk at violence to resist arrest. At first, they used boathooks, handspikes, whips and scythes but soon turned to cutlasses and firearms to protect their illegal cargos. A mob attacked customs officers with cricket bats, stones and staves as they attempted to apprehend a smuggling galley beached on the shingle in 1771.

Individual officers were targeted. One unenviable coastguard was pounced upon, trussed up in a sack and dumped to suffocate in St George's Churchyard. Another officer was left to dangle on the end of a rope over the moat at Deal Castle. A third was thrown over the cliffs at Kingsdown and dashed to pieces on the rocks below.

Local boats were custom built, either in England or France, with hollow masts for storing tobacco and false forecastles, bulkheads, bows or keels for concealing barrels of spirits. A favoured place for hiding contraband was in the cargo hold. Cabins held secret compartments behind panelling, under floorboards and above ceilings. Skeins of tobacco were artfully coiled to resemble lengths of rope. Fishing nets, ballast bags and beach huts provided further concealments.

Homeward-bound vessels of the East and West India Companies paused in the Downs, laden with spices, opium, sugar, silk and ivory, from the mid-seventeenth century. Their captains and crew were not averse to selling 'over the side' – a constant source of annoyance to revenue men.

Boatmen's clothing offered further opportunities for subterfuge. Pockets were stitched inside their clothes allowing jackets, waistcoats, trousers, even underwear to hold quantities of tea and tobacco. A 'duffer' might walk with these padded garments all the way to London where he found a ready market. Alas, tea was often doctored with liquorice, wood shavings or even sheep's droppings. City folk, ignorant of the refined taste of this expensive commodity, were most unwise to purchase 'duff' tea.

William Pitt, incensed at the loss of income from duties that funded coastal defences at the time of the French Wars, took drastic action to curtail the activities of smugglers. He ordered the destruction of sturdy boats employed by smugglers beached at Deal in 1784. Ironically, Pitt secretly received important information concerning Napoleon's activities from local smugglers while in residence at Walmer Castle.

Deal's former boatmen's quarter boasts an abundance of imposing properties that can only have been built on the profits from smuggling. Vast attics, secret rooms and connecting cellars reveal the extent of the illegal trade. When builders are employed to renovate period houses, smuggled goods themselves occasionally come to light. One intriguing discovery concerned a batch of two dozen ladies' French kid gloves, which were wrapped in oilskins concealed under floorboards in a house in Golden Street.

There is a suggestion that the word 'smuggling' derives from the Old English 'smuga', meaning hidey hole. On the first floor of No. 13 Silver Street there is a trapdoor in a recess to the left of the fireplace where a wooden ladder leads down to a compact hide on the ground floor. An enormous storage space was recently discovered behind the back bedroom on the top floor of No. 2 Farrier Street.

Renovation of No. 94 Middle Street showed a vertical drop behind the fireplace inside a ventilated cupboard on the first floor and a hidey-hole beside the chimney breast on the second floor of No. 151 Middle Street. The cellar of the former Seven Stars Inn (No. 142 Middle Street) was filled with shingle – an indication that it was discovered storing contraband. A large wooden box, possibly for concealment of tea or tobacco, was found by workmen under flagstones by the fireplace in the basement of No. 175 Middle Street.

Revenue men were unlikely to discover the extensive rooftop route stretching almost the entire length of the north side of Coppin Street. Artfully concealed, the smugglers' run, hidden by double-hipped roofs, allowed the gentlemen to pursue their illicit trade undisturbed, even when a search continued in the street below.

The start of the audacious hideaway lies at No. 5 Coppin Street where a slim wardrobe by the fireplace on the first floor conceals a secret rear compartment where smugglers might wait until the all clear. Access to the run is gained through a window on the top

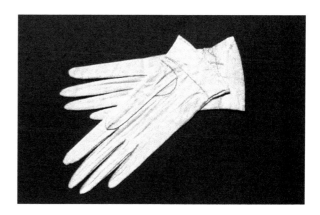

A smugglers' cache: ladies' French kid gloves.

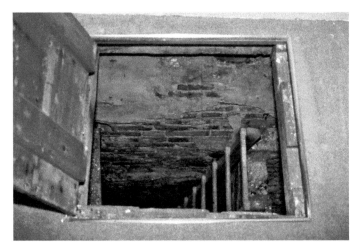

An upstairs hidey hole, No. 13 Silver Street.

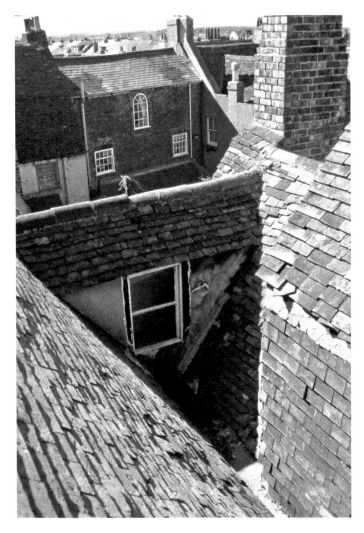

A window opening onto a smugglers' rooftop 'run' in Coppin Street.

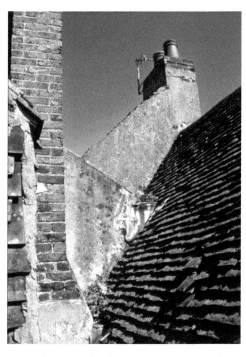 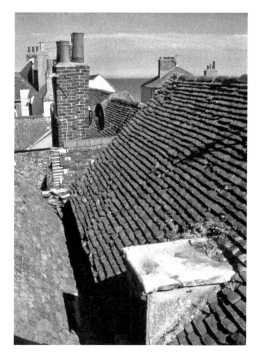

Above left: Steps leading to the rooftop 'run'.

Above right: A concealed narrow gully with an entrance into an attic.

floor where stone steps built into the opposite wall gives footholds leading to a narrow gully. This serves as a footpath running between the rooftops of several connecting houses where the smugglers deftly conveyed their goods. Trapdoors set into the roofs enabled contraband to be stored in the spacious attics. Occupants of these houses were denied access to their own lofts, which can still only be reached from the exterior. The exception is No. 7 Coppin Street, where an internal trapdoor allows access to an extensive loft. Here the treads are exceptionally sturdy to prevent tubs of spirits crashing through the ceiling. Thus, the artfulness of the Deal smuggler had reached its zenith.

Today HM Customs and Excise at Dover is responsible for preventing smuggling by ferries and pleasure craft in the English Channel. Smuggled goods now number alcohol, tobacco, drugs, pornography, firearms, ammunition and illegal immigrants. Counterfeit goods such as Swiss watches, designer clothes, DVDs and motor parts may be secreted in cars and lorries. In short, smuggling in Deal and Walmer has never actually stopped.

DID YOU KNOW?
After Lady Hales had offered her a swatch of chintz purchased as 'run' goods, Fanny Burney recorded in her diary (7 September 1778) that Deal was a 'sad, smuggling town'.

5. Goodwin Sands

Shakespeare mentions the Goodwin Sands in *The Merchant of Venice*: '...a very dangerous flat, and fatal, where the carcasses of many a tall ship lie buried' (Act 3, Scene 1).

Stretching roughly between the two forelands of the Kent coast, the Goodwins form two distinct sandbanks – north and south – bisected by an often traversable channel, the 'Kellet Gut'. These vast obstacles, mainly concealed beneath the waves, lie in the middle of the Strait of Dover – the narrowest part of the world's busiest highway, the English Channel.

This modest area of the Narrow Seas has been responsible for hundreds of wrecks and loss of thousands of lives, more than any other stretch of water around the coast of Britain. Lying 4 miles offshore – 12 miles long and approximately 5 miles wide – they have, until recently, proved impossible to chart. Over the centuries, the Goodwins, presenting such a hazard to shipping, have earned their dubious reputation as the 'Shippe Swallower'.

Attempts have been made to mark this perilous obstacle: two lighthouses (North and South Foreland), four lightships (a wooden vessel with three lanterns burning candles was placed at the North Sand Head in 1795) and, presently, ten buoys, whose twinkling lights present a code, incomprehensible to landsmen.

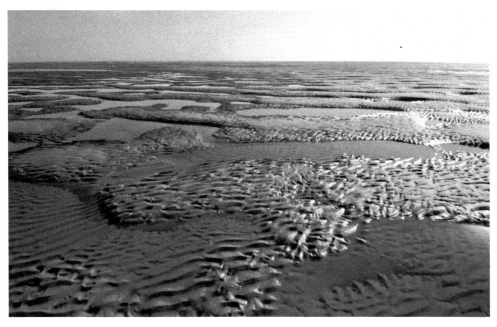

The Goodwin Sands at low tide.

Paradoxically, when the wind is in a certain quarter, the Goodwin Sands acts as a breakwater holding back the tremendous waves in the English Channel. It is said the rapacious Goodwins have saved a thousand ships for every one they have claimed. Indeed, the towns of Deal and Walmer owe their existence to the protection of these sands.

All manner of vessels have foundered there – Roman galleys, medieval cogs, sailing ships and pleasure steamers – but the number of wrecks can only be estimated. The huge expansion of mercantile trade in Victorian times increased incidents surrounding these perilous sandbanks.

In 1877, the celebrated tea clipper *Cutty Sark*, reputed to be the fastest clipper in the world and modified for the wool trade in Australia, experienced an alarming brush with Goodwins. Then in the twentieth century two identical ships, both named *Mahratta*, and both conveying tea from India, were wrecked on these Sands. In 1909, the first *Mahratta* became the largest ship to be claimed. She struck due to navigational error and, despite assistance from eight tugs and three lifeboats, she failed to refloat and split in half. Her sister ship, *Mahratta II,* ran aground thirty years later. Mahogany furniture from these two distinguished ships, inexplicably, graced elegant homes in Deal and Walmer.

DID YOU KNOW?
Burials have taken place on Goodwin Sands. Glanville, the brother of John Evelyn, the diarist, was laid to rest there in 1702 and Francis Merryditch, embalmed in a lead coffin, in 1751.

During the First World War, three German submarines were sunk by British warships close to the Goodwins. In 1917, the destroyer HMS *Liberty* rammed the *UC-46*; a British submarine torpedoed the *UC-63*; while the destroyer HMS *Gypsy* shelled *U-48*, which ran aground on the North Sand Head. Periodically, changes in the shape of the sandbank cause this last submarine to emerge and she becomes the object of divers, hunting for souvenirs.

Occasionally, aeroplanes too have been claimed by the Goodwins. On 18 October 1923, the engine of a Focker monoplane owned by the Royal Dutch Air Mail and being flown from Amsterdam to London, overheated and the Russian pilot made a forced landing on the Sands. He was rescued but the plane, along with mail and luggage, was lost. On 9 July 1940, Spitfires from No. 54 Squadron forced a Heinkel HE59 seaplane to land on Goodwin Sands. At that time the German seaplane was serving as an air ambulance, rescuing airmen from the sea after they were ditched.

A rare German bomber, a twin-engined Heinkel Dornier DO 17, known as 'the Flying Pencil', was raised from Goodwin Sands in the summer of 2012. This distinctive, double-tailed bomber was part of an enemy formation attempting to attack airfields when it was intercepted on 26 August 1940 and, despite the pilot's successful wheels-up landing, the plane sank. Half the camouflaged bodywork remains intact plus both propellers and

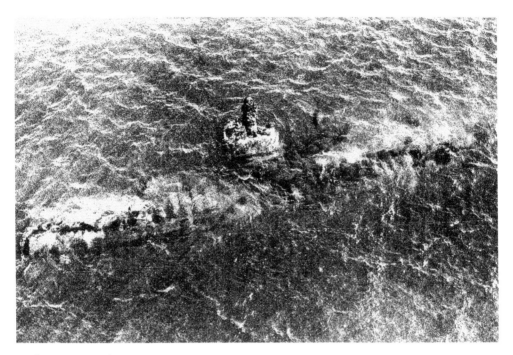

Sunken German submarine U-48.

the undercarriage – her tyres still inflated; however, neither the cockpit nor bomb bay have survived. After restoration, the Dornier will be displayed at RAF Hendon. It is an unprecedented survival from the Battle of Britain.

In the immediate post-war period, the English Channel was exceptionally busy with the transportation of foodstuffs, supplies and equipment to Europe by American Liberty ships. Administrators of the American navy unwisely declined to employ pilots to navigate these freighters since they deemed the additional expense uneconomical. Inevitably, an enormous number of accidents occurred, earning this part of the coast the name 'Calamity Corner'.

On 30 January 1946, the *Luray Victory*, bound from Baltimore to Bremerhaven with a cargo of cereals, steamed up Channel at maximum speed, oblivious of an impending storm. She struck the South Goodwins with such immense force she became a total wreck. On 13 September 1946, the *Helen Modjeska*, carrying foodstuffs, military vehicles and high explosives, bound from Marseilles to Bremerhaven, took a shortcut through Trinity Bay and foundered on the Goodwins.

On Christmas Eve 1946, the *North Eastern Victory* grounded near the East Goodwin lightship and swiftly broke her back. The crew were transferred to Walmer lifeboat while the captain and officers remained to salvage her cargo. The lifeboat crew waited patiently at dawn on Christmas Day to take the officers off, and ate turkey, drank rum and sang carols as the ship disintegrated. For a long time the tilting foremast and Samson posts of the sunken ship remained visible from the shore to testify that, once again, victory had gone to the sea...

Our worst post-war disaster occurred when the South Goodwin lightship (LV90) parted her riding cable and drifted from her moorings on the night of 26 November 1954. The lightship was swept rapidly south of the Kellet Gut where she capsized and lay on her starboard side, gripped by the voracious Sands. The crew of the East Goodwin lightship alerted the coastguard and although lifeboats from Ramsgate, Dover and Walmer attended, aided by Trinity House tenders *Vestal* and *Patricia*, they were all held back by the maelstrom.

An American army air force helicopter from RAF Manston located a sole survivor clinging to the light tower despite mountainous waves. He was a young scientist, monitoring migratory birds for the Ministry of Agriculture and Fisheries. All seven of the professional crew drowned and the lightship itself was rapidly swallowed by the sandbank. This was one of the first air-sea rescues to take place, and the pilot received a silver medal for his bravery from the RNLI. Trinity House, as the result of this tragedy, imposed a programme of replacing manned lightships with solar-powered vessels around the entire coast of Britain.

Radio Caroline's pirate radio ship *Ross Revenge* snapped her anchor chain and drifted towards the Goodwins during the early hours of 20 November 1991. Her caretaker crew slept soundly but awoke to the hull's grinding and raised the alarm on their VHF transmitter. Ramsgate lifeboat responded, plus a RAF helicopter from Manston that winched her nervous crew, including several disc jockeys, to safety.

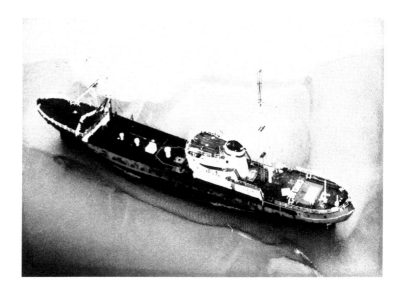

Radio Caroline grounded on the Goodwins.

At certain tides, the Sands are exposed and it is possible to wander across the hardened rippled surface, avoiding the many pools and gullies. Intrepid folk have organised a variety of eccentric activities including picnic parties, horse races, treasure hunts and firework displays. Among the sports played there are football, tennis, cycling, croquet, boules and golf, although the most frequent is cricket.

The first recorded match took place on 13 August 1813 when Thomas Elgar, with four friends from Ramsgate, challenged George Witherden and his team from Thanet. The latter won by a single run: 22 to 21. Winners and losers drank to the health of George III.

A second team of enthusiastic cricketers set sail from Ramsgate in the summer of 1824 under the direction of the harbour master Captain Kennet Martin. Risking high tide and quicksand, these intrepid sportsmen enjoyed a serious game with all rules strictly observed. One player achieved 67 runs. Play over, corks were drawn and the toast this time was to George IV.

A third match played in 1839 almost ended in disaster for the daring Deal youths who ventured forth in an open boat. Their sport was hugely enjoyed and refreshments followed from a well-stocked hamper. Storm clouds darkened the summer sky and the wind strengthened with alarming speed. Unwisely, the youths ignored the warnings of the boatman to make for the shore. Luckily, friends ashore raised the alarm and the terrified pranksters were rescued by a lugger.

Two elevens from Margate competed on this hazardous pitch in August 1844. The site chosen for this cricket match was adjacent to Captain Bullock's Refuge Beacon, an ingenious structure intended for the refuge of shipwreck mariners.

On 10 August 1854, a fifth match was arranged by two Walmer gentlemen, Thompson and Hammond. Twenty-four players were recruited, including Captain Pearson and the crew of a hovelling lugger, *Spartan*. Teams landed on the Sands in the late afternoon and play began in earnest. The game lasted until sunset, with the winning team scoring 57 runs. The party returned to the mainland by moonlight.

The 'All Blacks' touring team played a game of rugby on Boxing Day 1921. These superior players were taking a midwinter break when they decided to explore the Goodwins. They were ferried out by a trio of motorboats from Deal: *Golden Spray*, *Skipjack* and *Moss Rose*. The team returned to New Zealand, boasting they had competed in the middle of the English Channel.

Cricket was revived on the Goodwins in June 1959 when Alderman Eddie Butcher, mayor of Ramsgate, captained a team in opposition to his chaplain, Revd J. C. White. The novel event celebrated the 75th anniversary of the incorporation of the borough. The only spectators were inquisitive seals. The mayor's team won by four runs.

Yet another cricket match was attempted on 3 July 1975. Crews of the Royal Navy Survey Ships *Echo*, *Enterprise* and *Egeria*, after spending months charting the local waters, participated in a vigorous game dressed in quaint costumes. Two summers later Her Majesty's rowing boat, *Hannah Snell*, escorted Royal Marines (5 July 1977) out to play another match. At the interval a loyal toast was drunk to Queen Elizabeth II.

Kent cricketers made a surprising expedition to the Goodwins on 1 July 1985. A fleet of fishing boats transported spectators to the Goodwins in idyllic weather conditions. Kent XI challenged a Select XI, composed of members of cricketing clubs from around Thanet.

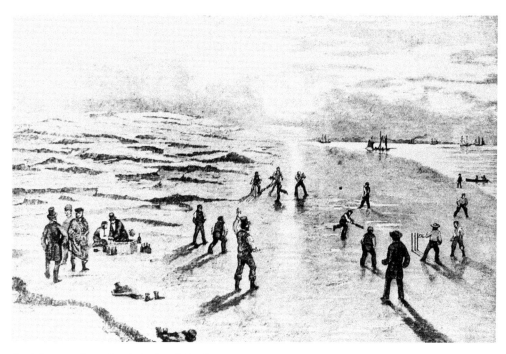

A cricket match on Goodwin Sands in 1854.

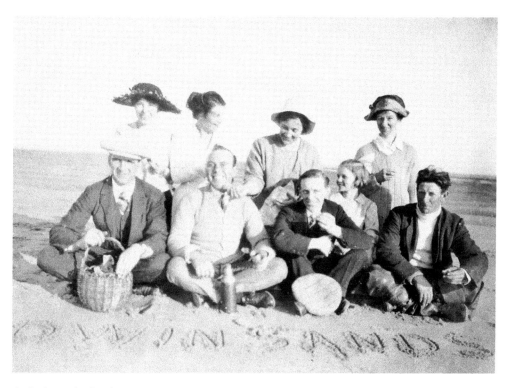

A picnic on the Sands.

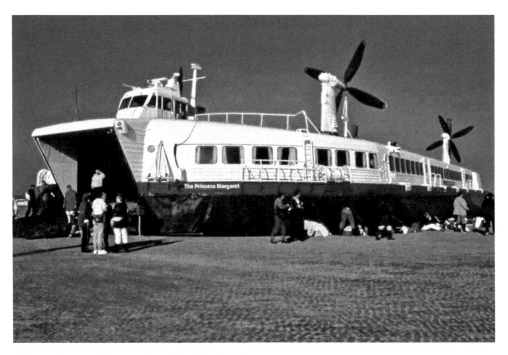

Princess Margaret hovercraft on Goodwin Sands.

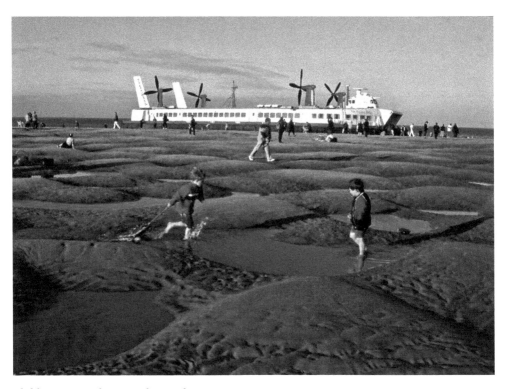

Children race toy boats on the Goodwins.

Their aim was to raise funds for a grandstand at the St Lawrence Ground, Canterbury. The captain of the Kent team, Chris Cowdrey, opened the batting, equipped with snorkel and flippers; but Derek Underwood, normally a deadly bowler, struggled with his own delivery. Stumps were drawn around 7 p.m. when both parties returned for a champagne reception at Deal Castle.

BBC's *Coast* recorded a cricket match in high summer 2006 while their presenter offered a commentary. Just as the tide began to turn, players were advised to leave promptly. As the film crew loaded their inflatable dingy with camera and sound equipment, they realised they were stuck fast in the sand. Stranded mid-Channel, the group waited anxiously until rescued by the Ramsgate lifeboat. The cricketers, later praised for their stoicism, had foolishly ignored their skipper's warning to 'make for the shore'.

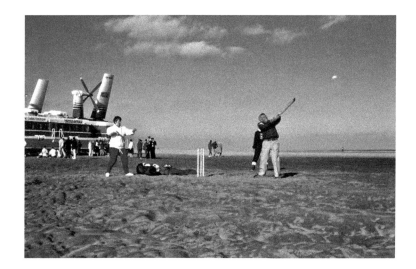

A modern game of cricket mid-Channel.

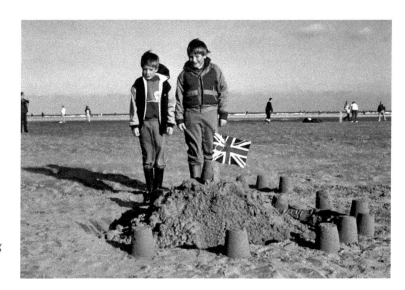

Sandcastles that will last until being consumed by the incoming tide.

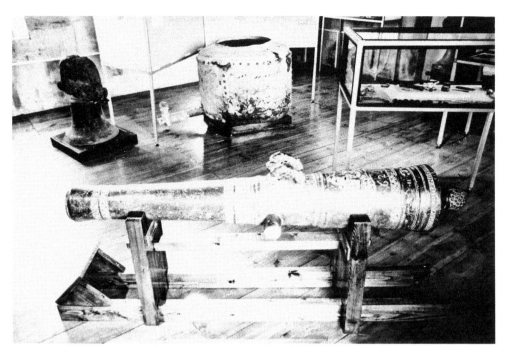

Dutch bronze cannon and ship's kettle raised from the wreck of *Sterling Castle*.

DID YOU KNOW?
A proposal was made in 2002 to convert the South Goodwins into London's third airport. There were to be four runways on two islands with a road bridge connected to the mainland. The Ministry of Transport turned down the scheme as its cost – £9 billion – proved exorbitant.

6. Deal Seafront

The Royal Hotel (*c.* 1720) is the last of a line of storehouses, boat sheds and quaint inns that once stood directly onto the foreshore. Originally, this was The Three Kings but it was renamed the Royal in honour of a visit from the German Princess Adelaide, future consort of William IV, the Sailor King, in 1818.

Vice Admiral Lord Nelson was a resident in the summer of 1801. Napoleon was assembling a vast flotilla along the French coast with which to invade England. Nelson was sent by the Admiralty to watch the harbours of Calais and Boulogne, lying directly across the Channel.

Nelson was suffering from toothache, enduring a heavy cold and was constantly seasick. He, therefore, chose to work at a shore base while returning to his flagship – first *Medusa*, then *Amazon* – at dusk. He planned a midnight command raid on Napoleon's shipping, employing special flat-bottomed boats built in the Navy Yard, which in the event went horribly wrong.

Nelson's ill-conceived plan was that four divisions of boats should row across to France at dead of night, maintaining strict silence and with muffled oars, but keeping close contact with each other. Their orders were to either tow enemy ships into the Channel and either sink them or set them alight.

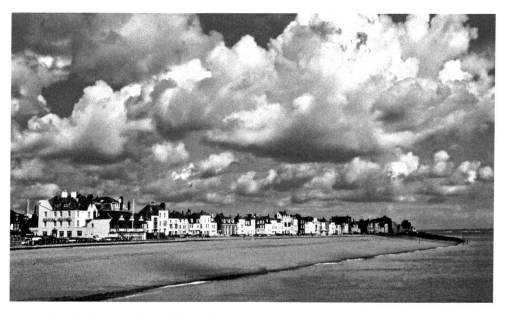

Deal seafront looking northwards from the pier.

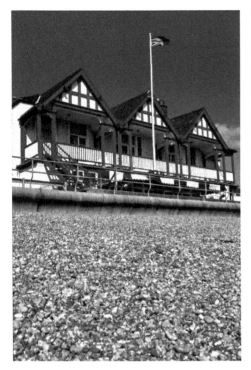 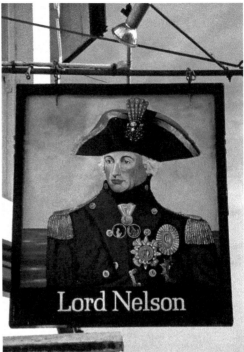

Above left: The Royal Hotel remains the only building directly on the foreshore.

Above right: The Lord Nelson inn sign, Walmer.

Napoleon, expecting subterfuge, doubled soldiers to sailors on board his ships, netted their decks and chained his vessels together so they could not be separated. Nelson's divisions lost contact with each other in the dark and in the bloody affray many of his best officers and men were killed or wounded.

Among the casualties was Nelson's close young friend, Captain Edward Thornbridge Parker. Terribly injured, he was lodged at a house in Middle Street – No. 73 seems right – where he was tended by the naval surgeon Dr Baird. Parker's leg was amputated without anaesthetic and thrown into an open pit at the adjacent churchyard. Three weeks later he expired in agony and his body was buried nearby, thus claiming the doubtful privilege of being buried twice in St George's Churchyard.

After weeks of being kept 'thumping in the Downs', Nelson was recalled to London, declaring the Downs a 'horrid bad station'. The Battle of Boulogne was Nelson's only signal defeat and is rarely, if ever, mentioned in modern naval textbooks.

Deal, on a happier note, has had three piers for residents and visitors to enjoy the bracing sea air of the English Channel. A Deal Pier Company was formed in 1838 and a plot of land was acquired just north of the Royal Hotel. Sir John Rennie, the celebrated engineer, was commissioned to design a wooden landing jetty 445 feet in length. Short Street, leading from the seafront, encompasses Wood Yard where spars and seasoned timbers for the construction of the pier were stored.

Sufficient funds to complete this ambitious project were lacking and the original design was abandoned. It remained, half its intended length, projecting from the foreshore, a constant hazard to boatmen. Finally, it succumbed to a storm in 1857. Stumps that formed part of the lower construction of this first pier are revealed during the lowest of neap tides.

During the mid-Victorian period the idea of a second pleasure pier was proposed by Edward Hayward, editor of the *Deal Telegram* newspaper. The new structure was designed by Eugenius Birch, credited with building over a dozen piers, including Blackpool and Brighton. It was 1,000 feet long and constructed of wrought and cast iron, and supported upon cast-iron columns screwed into the seabed. The abutment comprised stones from the demolished Sandown Castle.

There was seating along the pier's entire length and the stem was illuminated by globe lanterns, while a tramway conveyed holidaymaker's luggage. There were three decks – promenade, fishing and small boat – with a café and concert hall at the seaward end.

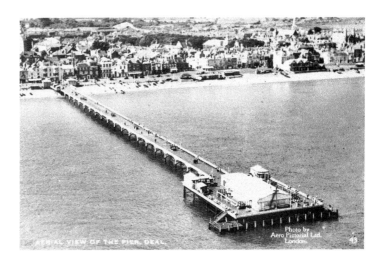

Deal's Victorian pier viewed from an early aeroplane.

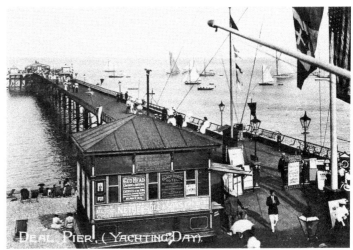

Deal's second pier on 'Yachting Day'.

The ceremonial opening, attended by the mayor and Corporation and accompanied by the band of the Royal Marines, took place in 1864. Mrs Fowler Burton, wife of the deputy commandant of the barracks, was the first lady to pay the toll and pass onto the new pier. A sudden squall resulted in gentlemen losing their top hats, but any distress was dissipated by a champagne and oyster reception in the new Pavilion.

Sea angling, which began in Ramsgate, soon spread around the coast to Deal where the new pier was an ideal venue. Here it was supervised by the pier master, Mr Lawrence, sporting a jaunty nautical uniform. He was replaced by George Rivers, a jovial figure with his pipe and faithful hound.

Tragedy struck the pier on numerous occasions. In 1871, the lugger *Reform*, after being launched in a gale to answer distress signals, was thrown between the piles and sank with loss of eight crewmen. In 1873, the barque *Merle* hit and damaged the structure, while in 1884 the schooner *Alliance* crashed into the pier, carrying away several columns.

On 29 January 1940, the Dutch ship *Nora* was struck fatally by a drifting enemy magnetic sea mine. A violent gale swept the crippled vessel northwards where she

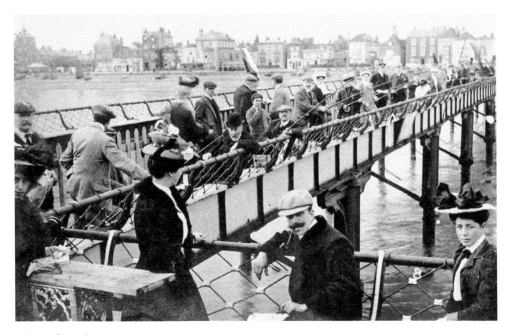

Fishing from the iron pier.

crashed broadsides through the iron pier. There she remained, a pathetic spectacle beached on her side, where youngsters enjoyed sliding down *Nora*'s bottom. The twisted remains of the damaged pier were blown up by the Royal Engineers on the orders of Sir Winston Churchill because they obstructed the field of fire from coastal guns after the fall of France.

Deal's present pier is built on the same site. Opened in 1957 by a young Duke of Edinburgh, it was the first pier to be built after the Second World War. Constructed of reinforced concrete, it has a 1,000-foot stem with open seating plus a three-deck pierhead. At promenade level there is a café, bar and terrace, while below the main fishing deck-cum-landing stage has angled wings to increase berthing facilities from pleasure steamers that frequently called in summer – the paddle steamer *Waveney*, and pleasure steamships *Eagle, Sovereign* and *Royal Daffodil*.

The Timeball Tower, which stands on the Promenade, was the earliest means of making Greenwich Mean Time known to shipping in the Downs anchorage. Its purpose was to signal accurate time – needed by mariners to determine their longitude – to fleets passing through the English Channel.

A first-time signal ball had been positioned at Greenwich Royal Observatory in 1833 to convey precise time to ships in London river. This early public time signal, erected under the supervision of John Pond, sixth Astronomer Royal, was so successful that a suggestion was made to provide one on the Kent coast.

Sir George Airy, seventh Astronomer Royal, was rowed around the Downs by Robert Wilds, later first coxswain of North Deal lifeboat. He decided that the former semaphore tower was suitable for displaying a new time ball. Subsequently, a black hollow wooden

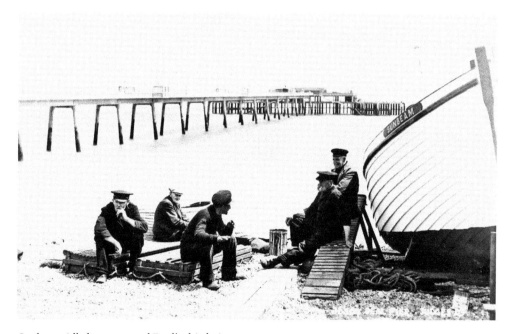

Sunbeam, idle boatmen and Deal's third pier.

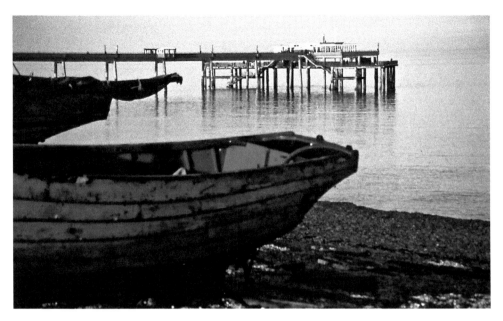

Deal's present pier viewed from the beach.

sphere covered with zinc, 5 feet in diameter, was mounted on a 14-foot mast surmounted by a weathercock. The connection by electric current was laid along the railway lines from Greenwich and the time ball was fully operational by New Year's Day 1855.

At 12.55 p.m. each day the ball was raised manually halfway up the mast; at 12.58 p.m. it was elevated to the summit and at 1 p.m. precisely it was dropped by electric impulse direct from the Royal Observatory. This signalled the precise time for ship's masters to adjust their chronometers before setting off on their precarious voyages worldwide.

DID YOU KNOW?
While Nelson was inspecting his fleet in the English Channel, the mayor and Corporation came on board his flagship to present him with the freedom of Sandwich. Nelson accepted the honour but politely declined to attend their invitation to dine.

Deal's time ball functioned perfectly, apart from when high winds prevented the ball being raised, until the tower was evacuated at the start of the Second World War. The Admiralty had recognised its intrinsic value and erected similar time balls around the coast from Edinburgh to Portland and several remain in Australia and New Zealand.

The first warden was William Newby, a naval veteran, who resided in the tower long past his eightieth year. A later warden was Isaac Hayward, founder member of Deal Fire

Brigade, who lived there with his wife and thirteen children. Last occupant was George Cutcher, retired marine lieutenant, who climbed with his family to the summit for their group photograph on the day the tower closed in 1927.

Deal was the first town in the entire world after London to relay Greenwich Mean Time. Until then each town had its own local time – Ramsgate was 5 minutes ahead of Deal – but this was finally superseded by the BBC broadcasting regular pips and later the GPO speaking clock.

Deal's Timeball Tower can be visited although its replica ball is now operated manually as a tourist attraction. After viewing a small museum dedicated to time and communication, visitors can climb the four storeys where powerful telescopes allow sweeping views of the Downs anchorage.

A Royal Navy Yard, which began in the reign of Charles II, stretched eventually from the Port Arms to Deal Castle and inland to Victoria Road. (It was then called 'Prospect

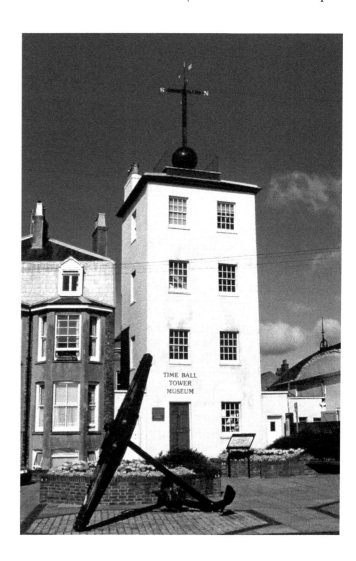

Deal's Timeball Tower.

Place' because its residents – captains, pilots and boatbuilders – enjoyed a view of the sea and even today several houses retain a nautical air.) It developed from modest beginnings for repairing and victualling the fleet becalmed in the Downs anchorage.

This King's Storehouse employed a vast number of workmen – shipwrights, blacksmiths, carpenters, coopers, chandlers, bakers, brewers, rope and sail makers – on land owned by the Archbishop of Canterbury. Although the Port Admiral, who inhabited his own a substantial property, was nominally in charge, the yard was administered by a 'storekeeper'.

Balthazar St Michel, brother-in-law to diarist Samuel Pepys, secured the position of muster master for the Downs Squadron. 'Balty' combined this office with Admiralty Agent for Deal, Dover and Ramsgate. He was succeeded by Thomas Warren, instrumental in completing this extensive Navy Yard on the south foreshore in 1703.

The Great Storm that swept southern England that November immediately devastated the new storehouses and boat sheds. Four great men-o'-war (*Restoration*, *Northumberland*, *Mary* and *Sterling Castle*) crashed onto Goodwin Sands with a loss of 1,100 brave seamen. The Navy Yard was slow to recover but once restored it served the Royal Navy for the next 160 years.

A later storekeeper, George Lawrence, was responsible for the expansion of the Navy Yard during the interminable French Wars. Storehouses were erected to house everything from signal flags to seamen's beds and workshops were constructed to facilitate essential repairs. Four steep slipways – some double – were built so high that a man might walk underneath them without removing his top hat.

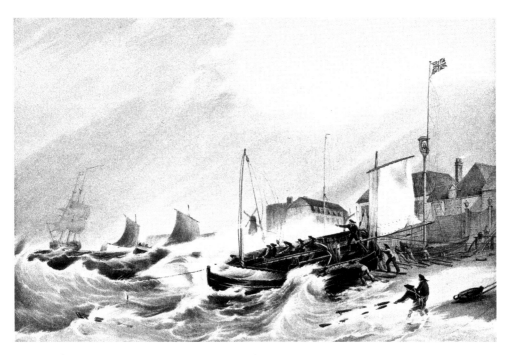

Launch of a Lugger from Deal's Navy Yard, painted by Henry Wise Harvey.

The Navy Yard eventually encompassed 5 acres and was enclosed by high walls on three sides with lantern-lit gates. At the northern entrance stood the semaphore tower that assisted the coastal blockade in the suppression of smugglers. One set of original gates graces the entrance to Felderland Farm at Worth, next to Sandwich.

In 1864, Deal's Navy Yard was closed, the stores removed to Chatham Dockyard and the land, excluding the Timeball Tower, was sold at auction. A residential estate, its tall villas present florid ornamentation including portrait keystones, coloured glass and painted tiles depicting flora and fauna, was built and named 'Victoria Town Estate'.

DID YOU KNOW?
Divers located the wreck of *Sterling Castle* on the North Goodwin and brought to the surface rare artefacts including a sailor's leather hat, a single shoe, the captain's pewter dining service, medicine chest, ship's bell, bronze cannon, a pair of rare copper cooking kettles and a candlestick clutched by a skeletal hand.

7. Walmer Strand

Royal Marines (soldiers that serve at sea) were formed early in the reign of Charles II. During the English Civil War the proportion of seamen to soldiers had fallen drastically. At the Restoration of the Monarchy in 1660, an attempt was made to redress the balance by James, Duke of York and Albany (later James II) who was then Lord High Admiral.

This new regiment of sea soldiers was known as the Duke of York and Albany's Regiment of Foote. Their uniform consisted of canary yellow, rendering them an easy target for snipers but in Victorian times their uniform was changed to khaki – a more sensible camouflage in battle.

Since their inception the Royal Marines have been closely connected with Deal and Walmer. It was not until 1861, however, that a permanent base was established in barracks previously occupied by the army. From the close of the Napoleonic Wars until the First World War, Royal Marines were rarely absent from active service, being engaged in the numerous battles accompanied by the expansion and consolidation of the British Empire.

The style 'Royal' had been conferred upon the corps by command of George III. Royal Marines, along with the Royal Navy, are accorded the privilege of remaining seated during the loyal toast. This tradition arose from their days served aboard wooden

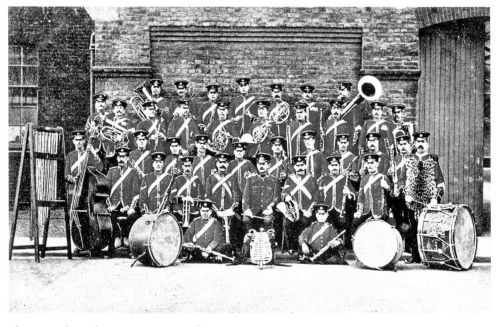

The original Royal Marines Depot Band.

battleships when there was little headroom between decks to stand and raise a glass for the sovereign's health.

Eventually, Royal Marines Deal Depot consisted of North, South (or Cavalry) and East Barracks. Originally a Royal Navy hospital, East Barracks remains an imposing building along Walmer Strand being 365 feet long with a sequence of sash windows, a central pedimented portico and a cupola containing a clock. It became the home of the world-famous Royal Marines School of Music.

The marching bands of the Royal Marines served Deal and Walmer with regular parades in summer, concerts in winter and by heading the carnival for the annual regatta. All ranks were measured personally for their ceremonial blue uniforms with red sashes and white helmets, thus ensuring they were always smartly turned out when in procession.

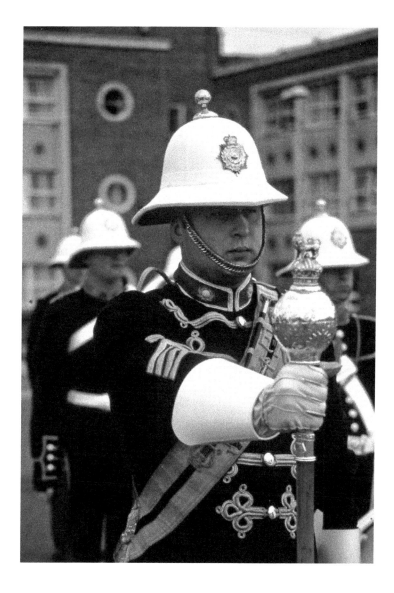

Sergeant major, Royal Marines Junior Band.

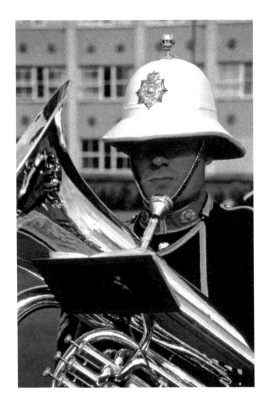

Bugler, Royal Marines Junior Band.

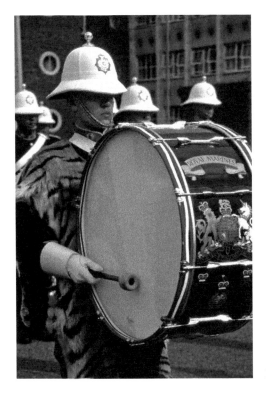

Drum major, Royal Marines Junior Band.

DID YOU KNOW?
During the Second World War the Royal Marines Siege Regiment manned two enormous cross-Channel guns (Winnie and Pooh) on Dover's White Cliffs, while 40 Commando trained at Deal prior to their epic raid on Dieppe in 1942. In recognition of their sterling wartime services, the freedom of Deal was conferred on the Royal Marines in 1942.

Sadly, following the detonation of a high-explosive bomb in North Barracks by the IRA in 1989, the Royal Marines were removed to Eastney, Portsmouth, in 1996. Thus ended more than three and a half centuries of association with the Royal Marines at Deal and Walmer. The extensive barracks of the last surviving Royal Marines establishment in Kent were converted into luxury apartments while a memorial bandstand to the eleven bandsmen killed still hosts open air concerts by visiting bands, including the Royal Marines, on Walmer Green.

The Goodwin Sands are so dangerous that eight lifeboats once served this narrow stretch of the English Channel. The first local lifeboat was placed at Walmer in 1856. She was a self-righter pulling ten oars, launched by carriage and named after the club that sponsored her, Royal Thames Yacht Club. Five years later she was replaced by a second, longer and heavier craft, also named *Royal Thames Yacht Club*, the first local lifeboat funded by the Royal National Lifeboat Institution.

Royal Thames Yacht Club combined its endeavors with a second lifeboat, *Van Kook*, placed at North Deal in 1865, to rescue the sailing ship *Iron Crown*, driven during a gale onto the Goodwins. The *Van Kook* (coxswain, Robert Wilds; second coxswain, Richard Roberts) was a rowing/sailing vessel, then the largest self-righting lifeboat in the RNLI's fleet.

A third lifeboat, *Onzio*, was added in 1866 under the cliffs at Kingsdown. Although the smallest in the RNLI fleet, this lifeboat arrived by steam train and was drawn to the village by six horses and forty boatmen. Her coxswain was Jarvist Arnold, a former Channel pilot who remained on duty for twenty years without deserved recognition. This corner of the Kent coast was then served by a sturdy fleet of lifeboats capable of launching in the fiercest storms.

All three local lifeboats were launched from an open, exposed beach. They were fitted out with twin masts bearing lug sails so that they could reach far beyond the Goodwin Sands, but they also carried a dozen oars since lifeboatmen preferred to row to their destination. Only the first thirteen men to answer the summons, don cork lifejackets and sealskin caps would secure a place aboard, but others were also required to hold greased skids in position to enable lifeboats to run down the beach at great speed and be afloat swiftly.

Communication between the three lifeboats, which launched according to wind and tide, was initially by a messenger on horseback. This system was replaced by maroons fired: the first signalled 'stand by', the second 'launch' and the third 'doctor required'. In response, shopkeepers along the Strand opened their back doors to allow crew members to take a short cut through their stores. Passing motorists might be flagged down to speedily drive more distant members to their lifeboat station.

When a third successive lifeboat, *Centurion*, came on station, a lifeboat house was built to shelter her on Walmer Green. Two further lifeboats followed (*Civil Service No. 4* ON 34, then *Civil Service No. 4* ON 394) before the dramatic decision was made to close Walmer station in 1912. It reopened in 1926 with *Barbara Fleming*, soon replaced by a fast, unsinkable motor lifeboat, *Charles Dibdin Civil Service No. 2*.

At the commencement of the Second World War, *Charles Dibdin Civil Service No. 2* was at the forefront of activity and frequently launched to assist vessels in distress despite the danger of magnetic or acoustic mines. She operated with extreme difficulty from a narrow gap in the barbed wire opposite the lifeboat house. After the fall of France it became impossible to man the lifeboat and safely enter the Downs anchorage. But with a Royal Navy crew she took part in the dramatic evacuation of Dunkirk. When she was retired after twenty-six years' service she had earned the reputation of being the busiest lifeboat in the world – she had launched 241 times and saved 412 lives.

When the Royal Navy gained control of the English Channel towards the end of hostilities, *Charles Dibdin Civil Service No. 2* gained a new coxswain, Freddie Upton. He became, perhaps, the most famous name in the history of Walmer lifeboat, serving from 1945 to 1962. In that immediate post-war period, there was an astonishing series of shipwrecks which, apart from the American Liberty Ships, included the Greek steamer *Ira* (1947), the Italian vessel *Sylvia Onorato* (1948) and the French freighter *Agen* (1952) which, because of heavy seas, broke her back immediately.

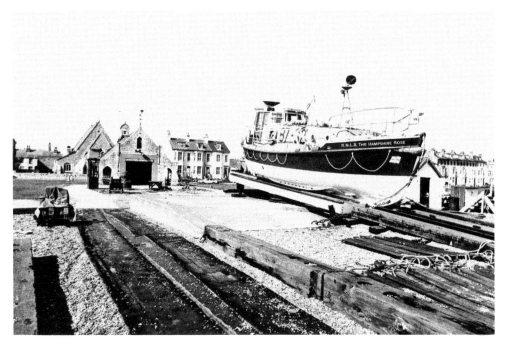

Hampshire Rose, the last Walmer lifeboat.

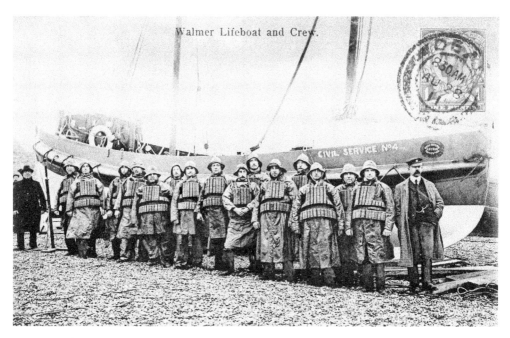

Walmer lifeboat *Civil Service No. 4*.

In 1975, *Charles Dibdin Civil Service No. 32*, a beach-type motor vessel, came on station at Walmer and served until 1975 (the 150th anniversary of the RNLI). Coxswain Upton was involved in Walmer lifeboat's all-night vigil when the East Goodwin lightship parted her riding cable and was driven onto the Goodwins. Three courageous coxswains followed in succession: Ben Bailey, Harry Brown and his nephew, Bruce Brown, the fourth generation of lifeboatmen in his family.

The last lifeboat at Walmer was *Hampshire Rose*, a gift of the people of Hampshire (and Sussex) whose county emblem is the rose, and launched by Lady Rose, wife of Sir Alec Rose, round-the-world lone yachtsman, in 1975. At the time she was only one of three beach-launching lifeboats across the country and among her rescues, listed on tally boards at the station (open regularly for inspection), are a cat and a dog.

DID YOU KNOW?
Walmer historian Revd Charles Elvin suggests that Walmer derives from 'gwal', meaning 'a site near a Roman fortification', and 'mer' meaning 'sea – thus 'the Roman fortification by the sea'.

The character of the lifeboat service in Kent has changed owing to the increased navigational aids and the service now operates mainly to assist pleasure rather than commercial craft. Present Walmer lifeboat is the offshore rigid inflatable Atlantic 85 *Donald McLauchlan*. Launched by tractor trailer, she carries a crew of five, including her helmsman. She is supported by the smaller D Class *Douglas Rodbard*, which deals specifically with inshore rescues. They arrived together in 2006 – the first time that two lifeboats arrived simultaneously and were named on station in the history of the RNLI.

An increase in the number of working boatmen at Lower Walmer in the early nineteenth century indicated it was necessary to build a convenient chapel of ease to Old St Mary's closer to the seashore. Champion of this cause was its vicar, Revd Henry Wilberforce, youngest son of William Wilberforce, who was instrumental in abolishing the slave trade. A subscription list for a new chapel of ease was opened and among the first subscribers was the Duke of Wellington.

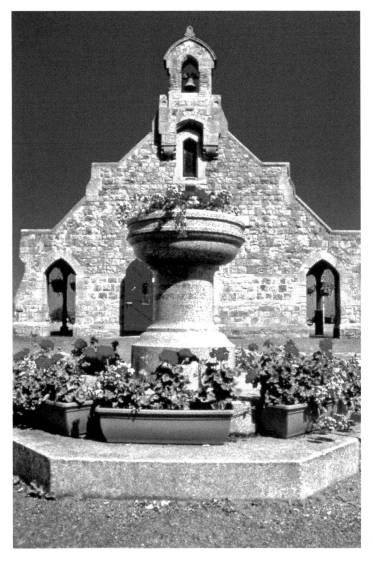

Walmer lifeboat station.

The foundation stone was laid on 15 August 1848 by Mrs Harriet Bridges, mother of the poet Robert Bridges who lived at Roselands in Upper Walmer. The following year the new ragstone building, consisting only of a nave, south aisle and small chancel with west and south doorways, was dedicated to the Holy Saviour by the Archbishop of Canterbury. (The north aisle was added in 1896.) The original contract for the new church specified that it should be built 'on the east side of the high road', which, if adhered to, would have meant that St Saviour's stood on Walmer Green.

The little church accommodated 380 worshippers, although by the time it opened the population of boatmen had dwindled. The east end, once brightly painted, focuses on Christ's crucifixion in its east window while an English altar presents gilded eagles on each of its four riddle posts. At the west end is an octagonal stair turret leading to steeply tiered pews in the children's gallery. The pulpit is peculiarly placed against the south abutment of the chancel arch and the entrance is contrived by means of an archway in the south wall of the chancel, making the preacher appear to leave the church and re-enter to deliver his sermon.

Surmounting the west gable was a tiny shingled spirelet containing a bell. During a thunderstorm on the morning of Sunday 10 August 1890 the church was struck by lightning, which demolished this belfry. The lad whose duty it was to ring the bell had only just left his post and escaped with his life.

Disapproval at the improvements to Old St Mary's, the parish church, resulted in a determination to build a more harmonious building to serve the discerning worshipping community of Walmer. Land was obtained atop Constitution Hall overlooking the Glen and building began in earnest.

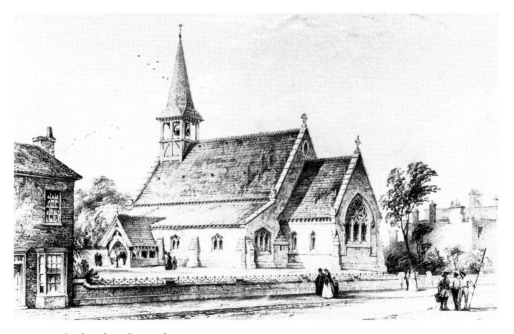

St Saviour's Church with steeple.

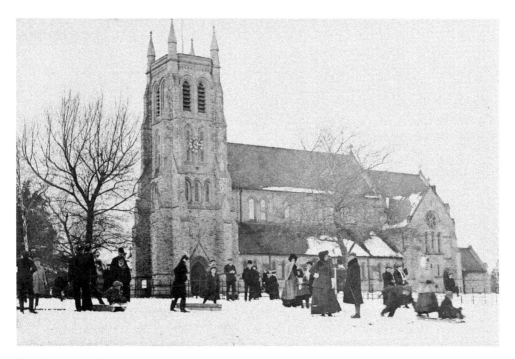

New St Mary's Church in the snow.

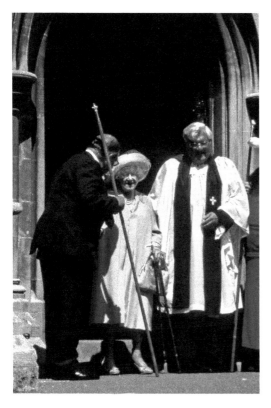

Queen Elizabeth, the Queen Mother, attends New St Mary's on its centenary.

New St Mary's, built of Kentish ragstone with Bath stone dressing from a design by Arthur Blomfield, was opened in 1888. It is in the Early English style and consists of a lofty, wide, spacious nave with arcades of five arches opening to its two small north and south aisles, a chancel and baptistry. The interior, which 'smacks of Victorian triumphalism', features a handsome reredos before the high altar formed of 'opus sectile', a form of mosaic composed of fragments of glass. Choir stalls are made of rare sequoia, which gives the church a rich, warm appearance.

Centenary of New St Mary's in 1988 was celebrated by the presence of Queen Elizabeth, the Queen Mother, Lord Warden of the Cinque Ports, while staying onboard HMS *Britannia*, anchored in the Downs. Revd Canon Bruce Hawkins preached the address when he remarked that 'instead of a congratulatory telegram from The Queen' his church was 'graced with a royal presence on its 100th birthday'.

DID YOU KNOW?
Services at St Saviour's were often disrupted when boatmen were called out to man Walmer lifeboat. The annual Lifeboat Service is still held at this church.

8. All Around the Town

High-speed trains from London to Deal, recently introduced, encourage visitors to explore this corner of the Kent coast. In Victorian times travelling by steam train across the county was an exciting, even daring, novelty. Charles Dickens ventured on the very first train to Deal. Later distinguished passengers included Lord Kitchener (in life) and the Duke of Wellington (in death).

Kent could boast it ran the first regular steam-drawn passenger train in the world. The Canterbury to Whitstable line opened on 3 May 1830 when twenty carriages were hauled along the 6-mile track by a sturdy locomotive: *Invicta*, built by George and Robert Stephenson (now displayed at the Whitstable Community Museum).

By the middle of the nineteenth century, a complex system of railways crossed Kent connecting London with the south-east coast. Their progress was chartered in Bradshaw's *Railway Guide*, a monthly timetable first published in 1841, showing Greenwich Mean Time rather than local times. Kent seaside resorts flourished from the constant influx of visitors, particularly after the Bank Holiday Act of 1871, which ensured regular holidays for all manual workers.

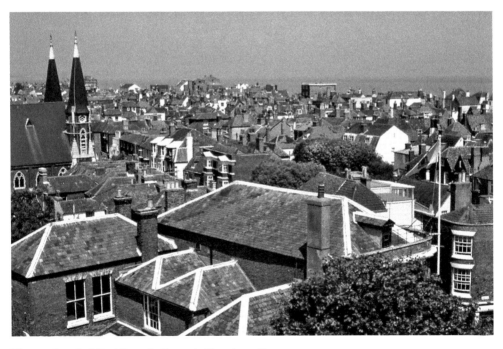

The north end of Deal from St George's Church rooftop.

Kent railways were operated by rival firms: the London, Chatham & Dover Railway and the South-Eastern Railway. The SER had brought its line from London to Dover in 1844. The same company also owned the Ashford, Canterbury and Margate line that reached Canterbury West, Ramsgate Town and Margate Sands by 1846. An 8-mile branch of that line across level farmland was opened the following year from Minster to Sandwich and Deal.

Transportation of the first steam engine to Deal almost ended in disaster. At that time lacking a swing bridge over the River Stour, an engine for essential railworks was mounted on a wagon pulled by a team of forty horses along the winding road from Dover to Deal. This extraordinary procession nearly came to grief when it slipped down a frosty slope at Oxney Bottom.

Engineer for the Deal to Minster line was George Robert Stephenson, nephew of the more famous George Stephenson. Deal station, the terminus of the new line, was built with an arched canopy over the platform and railway lines to shelter both passengers and trains. The station building, still recognisable today, consisted of a booking office, waiting room and porter's lobby with accommodation above for the guard and stationmaster.

DID YOU KNOW?
Creation of a coastal rail link to London resulted in the severance of the ancient Coffin Path linking St Leonard's Church at Upper Deal with the seafront. Consequently, a public right of way exists across the railway footbridge.

Opening of the coastal line from Margate took place on 30 June 1847 when SER Loco No. 37, *King Lear*, and its special, steamed into a crowded Deal station. Driven by the engineer, this was a tall, funnelled, six-wheeled engine, which drew a line of closed carriages. In Deal, shops were shut and businesses were suspended since the event was declared a public holiday.

A celebratory dinner took place that afternoon at the Town Hall. The guest of honour was Charles Dickens, who was staying with his young family at Bleak House, high on the cliffs at Broadstairs. He had been summoned urgently by electric telegraph and prepared a hasty speech, although no one knew what he was talking about.

The opening of the Deal line ensured townsfolk had a direct link with the capital city. It was, however, a tortuous route: the fare was exorbitant and the journey time took a laborious five hours. A proposal was therefore made to continue the line a further 8 miles to Dover, which came to fruition in 1874, a combined effort between the two existing companies. When the line was continued through to Deal it became necessary to build the overbridge, carrying vehicular traffic from London Road into the town centre.

To cater for the crowds of holidaymakers expected to travel to this popular seaside resort, the South-Eastern Railway commissioned James Brooks (an award-winning architect

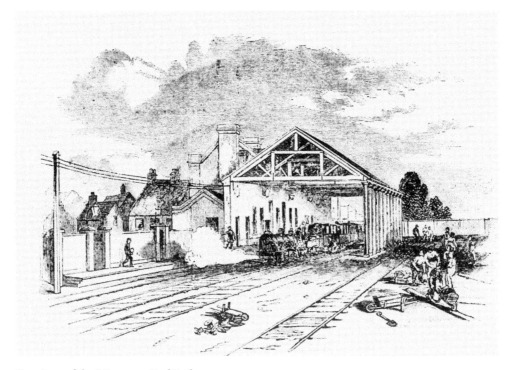

Terminus of the Minster to Deal Railway.

noted for church buildings) to design a sumptuous hotel along Victoria Parade. When the South-Eastern Hotel opened its doors to paying guests at the turn of the century, it was one of the principal features of the esplanade. Certainly, it was a dominating structure. It later became the Queen's Hotel, offering sixty-two bedrooms (some with bathrooms) a handsome staircase, tessellated tiled corridors and spacious public rooms. The seafront elevation boasted a grand central entrance flanked by twin conservatories that offered diners superb vistas over the Downs. On either side of the doorway were carved angels: one carried the town's coat of arms and a galleon, while the other supported the SER crest and a steam engine.

A bandstand stood along the seafront to entertain summer visitors in the late Victorian and early Edwardian periods. Built of cast iron with ornate valances, it was set in a railed garden with oval flower beds. Illuminated at dusk it looked enchanting. Military bands were hugely popular prior to the First World War, but the Royal Marines Depot Band drew the greatest crowds.

This prime site adjacent to the Timeball Tower offered further popular entertainment. There was first a roller-skating rink around 1920, before a covered Pavilion was opened by Lord Beauchamp, Lord Warden of the Cinque Ports, in 1928. This grand cast-iron and glass structure with canopied entrances along the seafront allowed for concerts and dances to be performed in all weathers, all seasons. The whole of the front façade could be opened to allow bright young things of the roaring twenties to relax on deckchairs, watching performances while still enjoying the sea air.

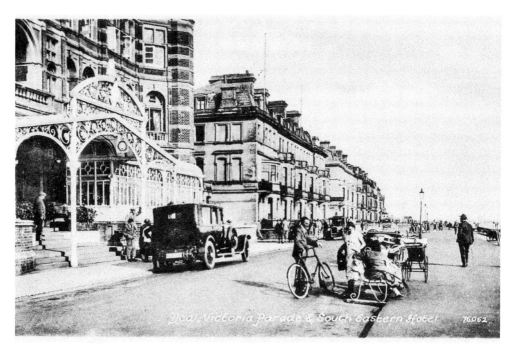

The grandiloquent Queen's Hotel.

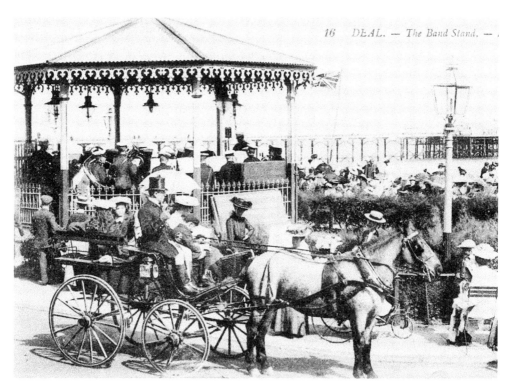

Victorian bandstand and iron pier.

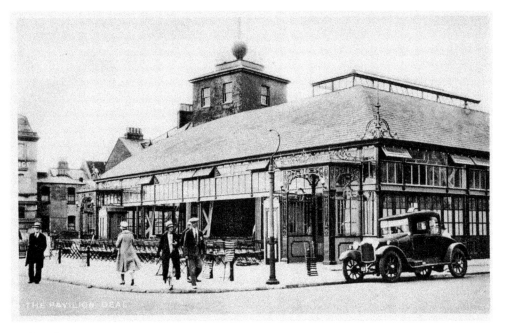

Deal Pavilion.

In 1933, the Pavilion was converted into a venue for novel talking pictures – the Regent Cinema. It presented a striking art deco frontage, seating for 900 patrons and opened with *King Kong*, which was shown repeatedly thereafter to British and American servicemen stationed locally during the Second World War.

Deal was originally a limb of Sandwich, which was regarded as the premier Cinque Port. When Sandwich Haven silted up in Tudor times, Deal rose to prominence as a town and port, served by the Downs anchorage. In 1699, Deal was granted its Charter of Incorporation as a 'borough and market town' by William III.

In 1702, a court hall, gaol and bridewell (or 'house of correction') was built in Deal's High Street. The building, which still stands between King Street and Market Street, was surmounted by a cupola, containing a fire and market bell. An early mayor was the fiery Thomas Powell, whose religious fervour earned him national notoriety in the reign of Queen Anne. He was praised by Daniel Defoe for his endeavours to rescue stricken sailors in the Great Storm of 1703.

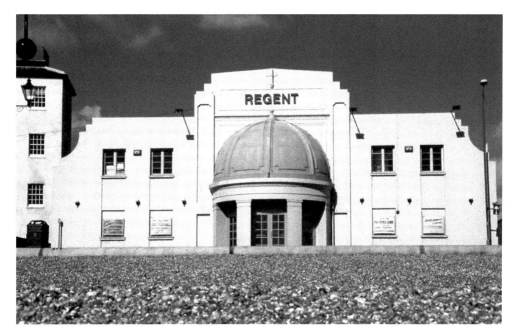

The Regent cinema.

In 1803, the present Town Hall was built in the High Street. It is an impressive brick structure with a central triangular pediment over a grand Venetian window. A row of stout Tuscan columns guard the forecourt, regularly the scene of a market, where formerly the town's fire engine was stored. At the rear were four cells, since Deal was originally policed by a town sergeant assisted by a dozen constables.

The Council Chamber is a noble, sunny room, graced with paintings of dignitaries associated with the town. There are portraits of William III, Sir Winston Churchill and Queen Elizabeth, the Queen Mother as Lord Warden of the Cinque Ports. Prominent is the painting of Deal's bluestocking, 'Mrs' Elizabeth Carter, wearing a borrowed gown and reading in a garden, by Joseph Highmore (c. 1758).

The Mayor's Parlour displays various treasures. In pride of place hangs the modest watercolour by J. M. W. Turner, *Deal in a Storm* (1738). Here, the artist achieves this dramatic effect by employing subtle pastel shades, and it is his only known painting to include a stroke of lightning.

The mayor of Sandwich, John Drury, was killed in a French raid in 1457. Successive Sandwich mayors have since that time worn black robes, denoting mourning, whereas Cinque Ports mayors wear scarlet. Deal's mayor, in sympathy, wears half mourning with a black robe and black bows tied to his gold chain of office. The only time this was dismissed was when Elizabeth I visited Sandwich in 1573 because Her Majesty refused to allow mourning in her presence.

In 2013, *Daily Telegraph* readers voted Deal as the winner of the High Street of the Year for its plethora of individual shops, cafés and restaurants. Occupying the old Sea Valley, the southern area was liable to extreme flooding until the sea defences were constructed.

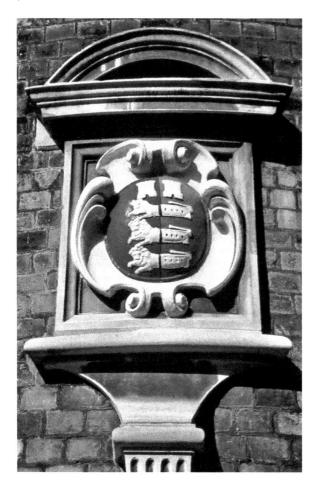

Deal's crest on the Town Hall.

It was once known as 'Lower Street', lying considerably lower than the seafront, and this is still indicted by several established businesses where customers step down into the interior to be served.

The oldest building in the town is the former General Baptist Chapel on the east side of the High Street, whose foundations mark the level of the Sea Valley. It was built (*c.* 1681) by Samuel Taverner, appointed captain of Deal Castle by Oliver Cromwell. A convert to the belief that all men are saved generally, he was later imprisoned as an insurgent in Dover Castle. The Gothic windows are modern but the interior preserves several ancient gravestones. Particular Baptists, who believe their members make a 'particular' response to God, later built their own chapel in Nelson Street.

Opposite, stands the dominant former Congregational Church (1882) now the Landmark Community Centre, with its twin piercing spires, 'Aspire' and 'Inspire'. In the modest graveyard is a pedestal monument recalling a reluctant cannibal, William Boys. He was cast adrift from the burning *Luxborough Castle*, homeward bound from Jamaica, and spent two weeks with a handful of survivors in the ship's yawl without food, drink, chart, compass, mast nor sail and forced to eat the flesh of his dead companions.

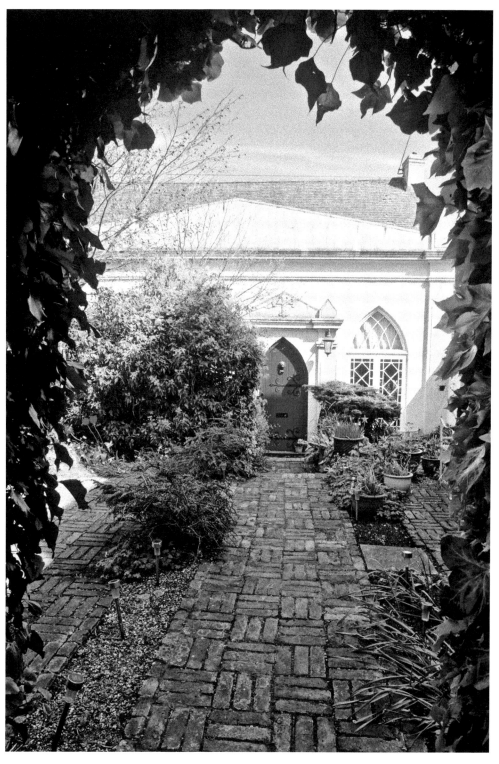

The General Baptist Chapel.

In 1774, Boys was made lieutenant-governor of the Royal Hospital Greenwich where he commissioned dramatic paintings of his ghoulish experiences (now discreetly tucked away at the National Maritime Museum).

Union Road, adjacent, led to the parish workhouse, a formidable building erected in 1796 that accommodated around 300 impoverished townsfolk. It closed in 1835 but the depressing site is still marked by Paupers' or Beggars' Alley, a straggling path bounded by a high brick wall on the west side of the present rectory for St Andrew's Church.

St Andrew's was opened in 1850 as a high church introducing colour and ceremony into the religious life of the declining seafaring population. Boatmen had seen steam replacing sail in vessels that allowed them to pursue their journey through the English Channel without pausing to take on provisions in the Downs anchorage. Their place in the community had been superseded by workmen employed by the new South Eastern Railway: engine cleaner, railway blacksmith, platemaker, switchmen, carman, stoker, porter, guard and gatekeeper, as recorded in church record books.

Built of Caen stone with a handsome tower and spire, it was immediately hailed as 'a decided ornament to the town'. Queen Adelaide, who held Deal in affection ever since she arrived in the port to marry the future William IV, had opened the subscription list but minor sums were collected from humbler maritime folk, now residents of the surrounding developing site, formerly devoted to market gardening. The chancel arch is uniquely formed as an upturned clinker-built boat while the stone lantern on the eastern exterior is shaped like a lantern to guide ships safely home to harbour.

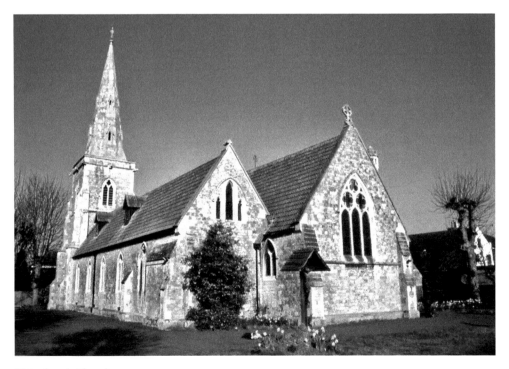

St Andrew's Church.

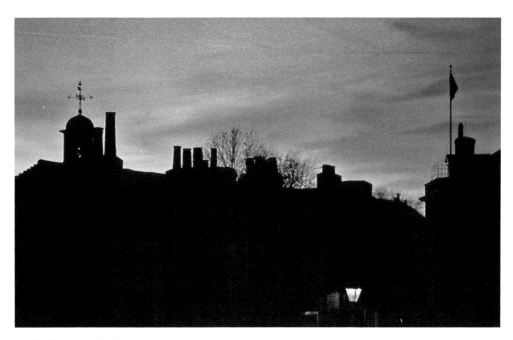

Deal's skyline at dusk.

DID YOU KNOW?
It is a peculiarity that whenever Deal's mayor boards a Royal Navy ship in the Downs, he or she automatically assumes the rank of Admiral.

9. Writers, Actors and Artists

Deal and Walmer have attracted a surprising number of actors, authors, artists and musicians who have found inspiration from their seaside surroundings. Several notable personalities had connections with The Beach, an area of exclusive homes at Lower Walmer, each with their enclosed gardens opposite.

John Hassall, pioneer of commercial art, was born there in 1868. His mother remarried after his father, Lieutenant Christopher Clark Hassall RN, died and his stepfather encouraged John's artistic talents. He specialised in children's book illustrations, theatre programmes, London Underground posters and trade advertisements for products including Veritas Mantles and Colman's mustard. His most iconic Edwardian holiday poster features a jolly boatman skipping along the sands with the caption: 'Skegness is SO bracing'.

The influential Roget family inhabited No. 13 The Beach. They are commemorated by lower panels in the huge west window depicting nautical scenes in New St Mary's Church, Walmer. Dr Peter Mark Roget was compiler of the famous *Thesaurus of English Words*, while his son, John Lewis Roget, was a celebrated artist who produced a superb book of local watercolours, *Sketches of Deal, Walmer and Sandwich* (1911).

Joseph Lister, pioneer of antiseptic surgery, spent a peaceful retirement at Coast House, No. 32 The Beach, until his death in 1912. A friend had recommended the 'bracing air

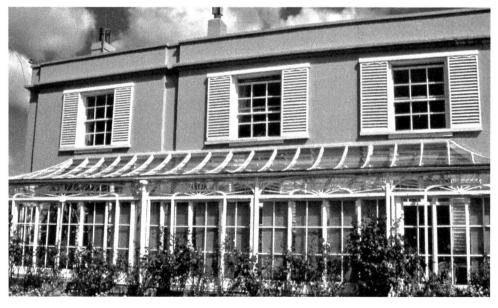

Coast House at Walmer.

and quiet attraction' of Walmer, and so he acquired, late in life, this grand house with its enviable sea views. Until he became an invalid, Baron Lister – he was the first doctor to be created a peer – enjoyed country drives and visits from younger relatives. On fine mornings he relaxed in a chair watching the sun rise over the English Channel and he relished the tranquility of this 'sleepy old Cinque Port town'.

DID YOU KNOW?
After the Second World War Noel Coward leased a house named White Cliffs, which was perched under the chalk face of St Margaret's Bay. 'The Master' entertained celebrities there and once brought close friends to watch the remake of his film *Bitter Sweet* at the Regent Cinema in Deal. Predictably, he hated it.

Dame Ninette de Valois, founder of Sadler's Wells, which became the Royal Ballet at Covent Garden, spent her childhood at No. 17 The Beach. Her real name was Edris Stannus but she adopted her grand stage name through a tenuous link with the French royal family. Born in County Wicklow, southern Ireland, she moved with her family to lodge with her wealthy grandmother who owned a large Victorian house at Lower Walmer.

The young Ninette was driven each week with her governess in a hired brougham to the Oaks School for Girls (later Tormore School for Boys) at Upper Deal. There she was taught gymnastics by a Royal Marines sergeant-major and classical ballet by an accomplished dance teacher from London. At home, on winter evenings, she would push back the heavily fringed armchairs in the drawing room to clear a small space where, by the light of the flickering fire, she would dance, accompanied by her grandmother, dressed in a stiff black moire gown, on an upright piano.

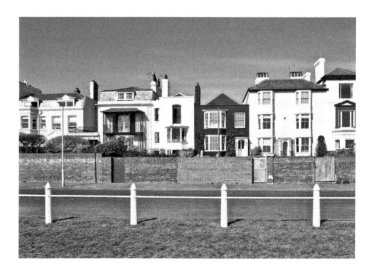

The Beach at Walmer.

Norman Wisdom and his elder brother Fred escaped from their brutish father in London and were adopted separately by caring families in Walmer. Norman lodged with Mr and Mrs Blanche, who lived in Downs Road, and was educated at Canada Road Junior School. To earn pocket money, he acted as unofficial porter for passengers arriving by steam train at Deal railway station, but later he gained employment as an errand boy for Lipton's, the grocers, in the town centre. He was thrilled to find a bicycle came with the job!

As a boy he had joined Walmer Sea Scouts. One day while strolling home in his uniform, he noticed a film crew rehearse a scene that focused on Walmer lifeboat. Entranced, the impressionable lad returned much later, slipping unnoticed out of his top bedroom window, to watch the friendly actors record a night-time scene where the lifeboat battled against rough waves. Forever after this popular comic actor, singer and musician who often returned to visit relatives now settled in Deal, acknowledged that he acquired his first taste of show business at Walmer.

Norman Long, a popular performer between the wars was the first entertainer to become a star by radio. He was born in 1893 above his father's shoe shop in Deal High

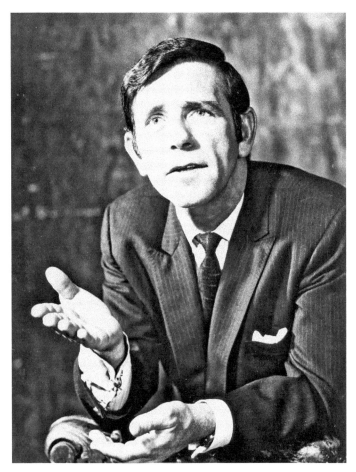

Norman Wisdom spent his childhood at Walmer.

Street. During the First World War, Norman found a talent to amuse soldiers in his regiment by composing songs that were first broadcast via the 'cat's whisker' in 1922.

This cheeky comedian was billed initially as 'a song, a smile and a piano', but this was later changed to 'a song, a joke and a piano' since a smile was difficult to discern on radio, though this did not prevent him from performing mystifying card tricks. Norman was proud to be invited to appear in the first Royal Command Performance on radio in 1927.

John Ireland, composer, rented a flat at Comarques (a Georgian house in the High Street) for a period prior to the Second World War. He regularly made the tortuous journey by steam train from London. His landlady recalls this shy, solitary man spent long hours secreted in his study writing music 'without a sound coming from the piano, other than an occasional chord'.

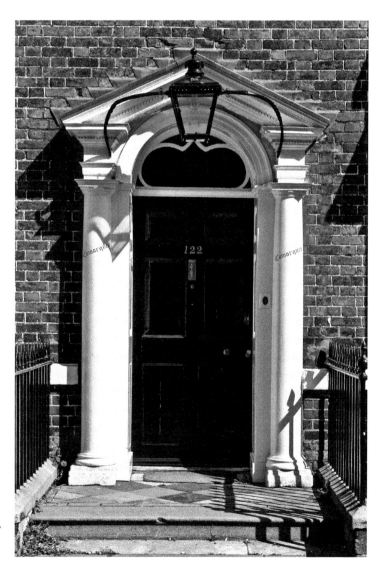

Doorway to Comarques, home of composer John Ireland.

At Deal he wrote a short piece for string orchestra, 'Concertino Pastorale', although his most acclaimed piece, 'Sea Fever', composed locally, incorporates words by John Masefield. His friend, Herbert Brown, a solicitor, attempted a biography but found Ireland reluctant to reveal personal details and so he abandoned the project.

Comedy actress Dorothy Summers owned a seafront café called, appropriately, Mrs Mopp's. She was the irrepressible charlady in the wartime radio hit show *It's That Man Again* (ITMA). 'That man' referred to Adolf Hitler. Tommy Handley starred as the mayor of a disreputable seaside resort, 'Foaming-at-the-Mouth'. Each episode featured a bizarre group of characters who entered merely to converse with him. They would each utter their familiar catchphrase, speak a few more lines, then exit abruptly.

Miss Summers, who played the charlady Mrs Mopp, would call out in her strident voice above the clatter of her iron bucket, 'Can I do you now, sir?' Families would gather round their wireless sets to tune in avidly in the wartime blackout. The show ran from 1939 until 1949, when Handley died, after which Dorothy retired to run her cafe at No. 81 Beach Street.

Jimmy Edwards, known for his trademark trombone and handlebar moustache, was famous for his roles as Pa Glum in radio's *Take It From Here* and the irrepressible Professor in television's *Whack-O*. Reluctantly, he spent one summer teaching at St Clare's, a preparatory school for boys (later Leelands) at Walmer in 1938. He began to lose confidence as he cycled from the train station, wobbling with his suitcase, on the first day of term...

Jimmy looked far too young so the headmaster advised him to acquire a trilby to distinguish him from his pupils. He could never keep discipline. 'The angrier I got the more the pupils laughed', he recalled, although he amused the boys by flying their model aeroplanes and supervising their swimming lessons at the Royal Marines Swimming Baths. His brief teaching career was a disaster, which is ironic since he made his fame as a rascally headmaster in radio, television and films.

'Big Chief I-SPY' Arnold Cawthrow lived for a time in the converted Boatmen's Rooms at the top of Exchange Street. The forty pocket-sized volumes, published originally by the

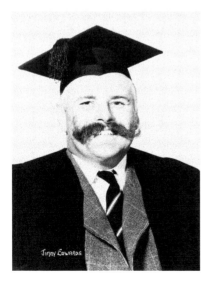

Jimmy Edwards was a teacher at St Clare's School, Walmer.

defunct News Chronicle, were popular with children in the 1950s and 1960s. Their titles, ranging from *I Spy at the Seaside* to *I Spy at the Zoo*, required young observers to spot objects on a theme for fake feathers to add to their American Indian headdress.

J. B. Priestley, playwright and novelist, spent one summer with his family in the rented house of Wardley, located along the Marina in north Deal. He found it convenient for visiting his sister who owned a tea shop opposite the Royal Hotel (now the Golden Hind bookshop). Priestley was delighted by his furnished property and wrote: 'For the past two months we have been living at the very edge of the sea.'

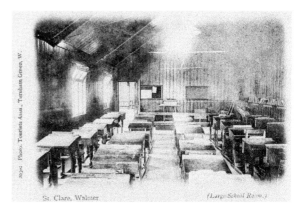

The classroom where Jimmy Edwards taught for one term.

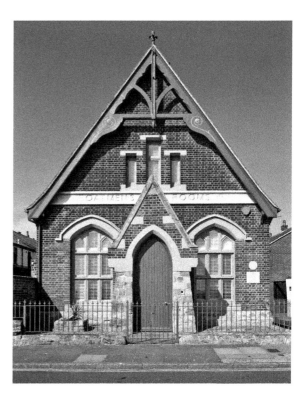

The Boatmen's Rooms became the home of I-Spy's Big Chief Arnold Cawthrow.

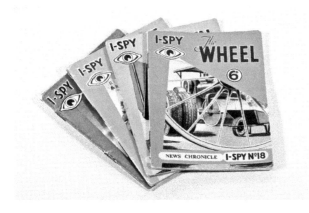

An assortment of early I-SPY books.

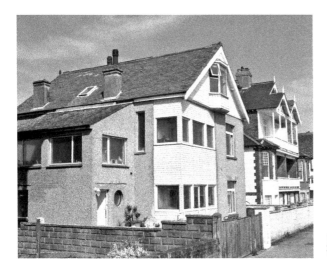

J. B. Priestley's holiday home,
Wardley, along the Marina.

Priestley completed his novel *The Good Companions* (1929) while at Deal. This frothy tale, later dramatised, caught the imagination of the reading public and became an outright bestseller. His story follows the adventures of a troupe of Pierrots travelling around the English coast in the 1920s. Priestly's description of the quaint seaside town of Sandybay seems familiar: 'it was still a fishing village, higgledy-piggledy of boats, nets, capstans, blue jerseys, mahogany faces and queer inns...'

Romantic novelist Victoria Holt, who also wrote historical novels under the pseudonym Jean Plaidy, roamed this area searching for inspiration for her plots towards the end of the 1960s. London born, her real name was Eleanor Hibbert, as a prolific author she wrote over 200 titles and sold over 100 million books worldwide. She stayed with friends at a converted public house, the Scarborough Cat (a 'cat' boat is a large lugger), on the seafront before purchasing the King's Lodging at Sandwich. From the top windows she observed the Goodwin Sands and absorbed tales of shipwrecks during winter storms and the heroic rescues of the Deal boatmen. Her research gave her the inspiration for an intriguing Gothic novel, *The Singing Sands* (1969), which focuses upon the notorious Goodwins.

The name of one film, television and radio personality that took up residence in Deal still causes a strong reaction among local inhabitants. Charles Hawtrey, star of the interminable 'Carry On...' series of cinema comedies brought a property on a whim in the conservation area in 1970. The capacious Georgian terrace house of No. 117 Middle Street was described in *The Times* as 'a warren of tight passages, stairs that need careful mounting and odd little cupboards and nooks'.

Born George Hartree to working-class parents in West London during the First World War, he encouraged the fantasy that he was the son of the actor/manager Sir Charles Hawtrey. The comedian had enjoyed a distinguished early career as the boy detective in radio's *Norman and Henry Bones* and Private Hatchet in television's *The Army Game.*

Hawtrey, resentful that his fame was based largely upon his interminable appearances in the 'Carry On...' films, which he despised because of its pitiful fee, brought his bitterness to Deal. Here, he was shunned through his aggressive alcoholism and dubious lifestyle. Eccentrically dressed in a floppy hat and long black coat buttoned at the back, he further failed to endear himself to the local community by refusing to sign autographs.

Kenneth Williams, in his own vitriolic style, records a fleeting visit to his friend on Sunday 10 May 1970 in his own posthumously published diaries. He found Hawtrey still unshaven when he conducted Williams around his period property, which retained a 'revolting smell of rising damp and cat's fish everywhere'.

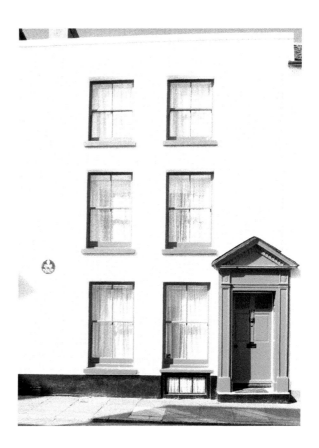

Charles Hawtrey's home in Middle Street.

Cabaret artiste Joy Leonard recalled a happier occasion:

One afternoon Charlie invited me round to tea. He was so proud he had made a trifle. It was all squirty cream with those break-your-teeth silver balls sprinkled on top. Sitting in one corner was Hattie Jaques. 'Come to the table', he ordered. 'Tea's ready!' But Hattie, being a big lady, was stuck in her corner chair. Charlie and I tugged and tugged her. Eventually, she fell forward on top of both of us, the chair still clinging to her bottom with its legs in the air. We collapsed in peals of laughter.

DID YOU KNOW?
In 1952, Ian Fleming acquired White Cliffs and set several escapades for his spy novels locally. James Bond Agent 007 confronts the megalomaniac Hugo Drax in *Moonraker* (1955) who builds his own atomic research centre on Kingsdown Cliffs and plays a round of golf with the arch-villain in *Goldfinger* (1959) at Royal St Mark's (actually St George's) at Sandwich.

10. A Stroll Along Middle Street

Carter House is a pleasing pink confection converted from four cottages in the eighteenth century by Deal's most illustrious inhabitant 'Mrs' Elizabeth Carter. Elizabeth, the favourite daughter of the intolerant Dr Nicolas Carter, was renowned as a scholar – remarkable for a woman in the Georgian age – and taught herself nine different languages. She rose to international fame when she translated the work of the obscure Greek scholar Epictetus and, as a member of the literary 'bluestocking' circle, she became the friend of the lexicographer Dr Samuel Johnson and minor royalty, several of whom visited her here.

The house with its modest garden, once ablaze with roses, myrtles, geraniums and honeysuckles, stands at the corner of South Street and Middle Street, formerly the haunt of the press gang and smugglers. The area, once composed of a hotchpotch of boatmen's homes and quaint inns (now desirable residences), is often alluded to as 'Little Chelsea'.

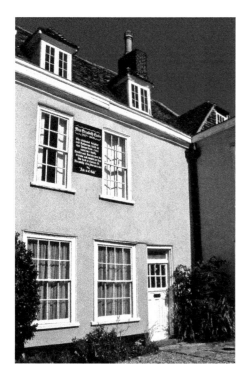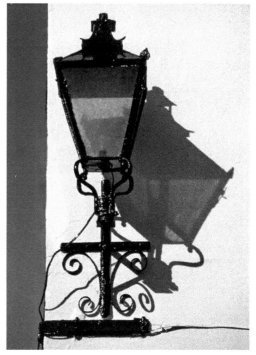

Above left: Carter House, home of Deal's celebrated blue stocking, 'Mrs' Elizabeth Carter.

Above right: An original gas lamp.

And it invites exploration. Its period features number gas lamps, gables, catslide roofs, foot scrapers and herring hangs. Interiors, too, are often pine panelled with winding staircases, powder closets, wig cupboards and hidey holes.

The first house one encounters, No. 2 Middle Street, is a perfectly preserved town house of the early Georgian era. Its furnishings and decorations are authentic for the period, including the arsenic green painted panels of the living room and muted mustard walls of the master bedroom. It is often hired for television and film locations.

There is an intriguing detour at Crown Court. Pass under the archway to investigate the boatmen's cottages and sail lofts in the little lane that leads behind the King's Head to the seafront. Once gaslit, this area was dark, gloomy and redolent of atmosphere.

No. 8 Middle Street bears a Deal Society blue plaque informing this was once the home of Miss Catherine Boys (1808–72). Charitably, she opened the Deal Orphanage for fifteen young girls in the mid-Victorian period.

Stonar House is a Georgian red-brick house whose door has a carved entablature featuring a pair of lions and an urn under a triangular pediment and a double row of five sash windows. Look for ancient graffiti carved in the brickwork, and below a windowsill the date '1780'.

Queen Anne House (1710), built of mellow red brick, stands back from the road with a neat garden protected by wooden palings and a gabled brick bakehouse. Perfectly symmetrically, the property has a central door with original brass fittings and a profusion of curiously unrecessed sash windows on two floors plus four shy dormers peeping through its Kent-tiled roof. A flemish gable in its southern wall matches that of its neighbour, whose end wall conceals a bricked-up window to avoid the despised window tax. It carries a 'Historical Building of Kent' plaque.

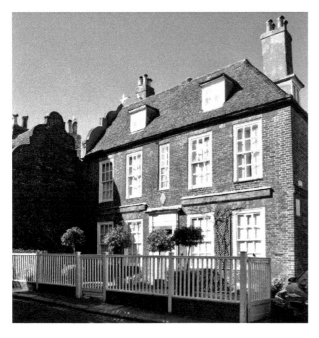

Queen Anne House.

Step down into South Court. Locals refer to it as 'Jaw's Harp alley' – its shape resembles the modest musical instrument. Properties in this hidden area reveal little sign of its former shady past, apart perhaps from the corner house once occupied by the local hangman. (The corner window displays its present owner's library of books, all with the title 'Hangman'.)

On the corner of Middle Street and Broad Street stands the former Roxborough Castle, which once hosted the annual dinner for the Deal Boatmen Club and for a time was the annexe to the seafront Pier Hotel.

A central area of Middle Street was bombed during the Second World War and is now a car park. The myriad lanes and alleys that remain tell of its historical past. Black Horse Alley has a side lane alongside the former slaughterhouse, while Cockle Swamp Alley indicates where sellers of shellfish disposed of their catch. Between them lies Coach Yard where proprietors hired out an assortment of vehicles – coaches, flies and bath chairs.

Primrose Hill leads under double arches and perfectly frames a view of the pier. Romantically named, it is thought this paved alley may originally have been the start of Church Path. At one corner is an icehouse where blocks of ice kept produce cool before the invention of refrigerators.

Custom House Lane, in two halves led to the Customs House, initially in Middle Street but rebuilt in the High Street in 1810. There were frequent attempts by miscreants to blow up the building and retrieve their confiscated contraband.

Five Step Alley led to the Boatmen's Rooms, now a domestic dwelling, on the seafront. Beamed and panelled, the rooms offered a place of relaxation for retired boatmen. They were furnished with hurricane lamps, fishing tackle, glass floats, a seaman's chest, a compass, scales, charts, a stuffed chub in a glass case and a supply of the day's newspapers. Pause to admire the cluster of immensely tall chimney stacks beyond its exotic walled garden.

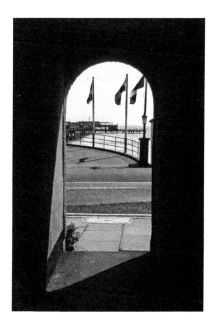

A glimpse of Deal Pier.

The Royal Cinema, which began life as an Oddfellows Hall, became the Theatre Royal, a venue for plays and concerts. In 1913, it was acquired by Charles Collins who added electric lighting, tip-up seats, cinematograph projectors and a large screen in preparation for the advent of silent movies. The first talking picture was *All Quiet on the Western Front.* The cinema remained open throughout the Second World War, but the advent of television finally closed our 'Royal'. The building retains its art deco chrome door handles, stills boards and a glass etched mural of a Hawaiian scene (boarded up).

Market Street takes its name from the vibrant fish market that was held behind the original Town Hall in the High Street. You can still see the flagstones where the baskets of sprats and herrings were tipped out for sale. The imposing Blackburn Hall, with its crinoline style doorway, once housed an eclectic museum. Chapel Street links with St George's Passage, and both refer to St George's chapel of ease. The proximity of the Three Kings (now Royal Hotel) to the church indicates that Lord Nelson and Lady Emma would have walked along here to attend divine service... and also why No. 73 Middle Street is proposed as the lodging for his sick friend, 'poor, dear little Parker'.

Next door, the Five Bells Inn has become a private property. Opposite, workshops too have been cleverly converted into residencies, but they can be recognised by their names: Oakwood, Dovetail and Spokeshave cottages.

The Royal Oak, situated on the site of the present car park, presented musical concerts and elegant balls and also hosted the curiously named Catch Club. Deal's mayor and Corporation frequently walked in procession along Oak Street to dine at the inn, which was conveniently near the Town Hall. A H-bomb fallout shelter was constructed within the pub's derelict cellars in the 1960s. The attractive Fish Bar opposite was once the Harp, and is still famed for its excellent suppers.

Next door was the National School for Infants, which was begun in early Victorian times and was known locally as 'Feed My Lambs'. Pupils were summoned by a brass bell in the little belfry. Behind lay a soup kitchen that in the last war became a British restaurant. Opposite was the Paragon (later Empire) music hall, which had a dubious reputation, but for a small fee a 'grand array of London talent' could be enjoyed there. It had seating in the stalls and circle, but there were also boxes, bars and dressing rooms behind the stage. Ladies were not admitted unless accompanied by a gentleman.

Between Brewer Street (named after John Brewer, Deal's first recorder) and Coppin Street (named after Joshua Coppin, Deal's first mayor) lies Vane House, a substantial Georgian property with a carved name plaque and a distinctive weathervane on the wall of its courtyard.

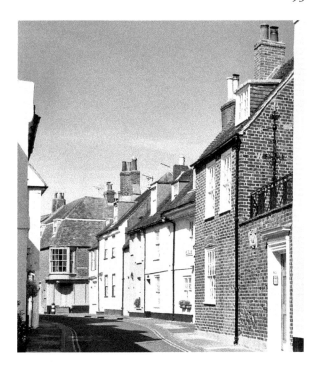

Vane House, looking towards the
'Old Stores'.

Next door is Fleet House, showing dental cornicing – a true Georgian feature. At one time Able's boatbuilder's workshop was located here. Notice the chamfered corner of the house opposite; this was to allow the newly built boats access to the beach.

A superb oriel window peeps out from below its mansard roof of the Old Stores (remembered as a gun and fishing tackle shop), allowing the occupants an enviable three-way lookout. Redan (No. 102) is an imposing property that once belonged to Sir Ernest Justice Charles, a high court judge and local benefactor, the garden of whose seafront home, Bruce House, adjoined. Its rendered exterior retains its ale boards and wide doorway that indicate it was formerly an inn – the Clifton.

The top end of Farrier Street has a superb trio of tall town houses, one of which bears a sweeping stone sign: 'Esperanza'. A puzzling red-brick property (No. 19), which has an impossibly tall doorway, blocked-in windows and arches was once the Horse and Farrier public house. Melbourne House, twisting around Middle Street, seems a pretentious property with its triple-canopied doorway and double-bell pushes – 'Visitors' and 'Servants'.

In this vicinity are former shops and inns that speak of a vibrant past. The Tally Ho (No. 118) retains its decorative ale boards, while opposite is another curious property (No. 127) with myriad filled-in doors and windows. Notice the patch of original cobbles and street paving stones – rare survivals. A short detour into New Street reveals a former storehouse with hoist, foot scraper and grimacing 'Jeremiad'.

A private house in Middle Street (No. 126) has its brick oven visible on the exterior wall around Golden Street, but opposite the Victorian postbox has sadly lost its original enamel sign. At the top of this street a superb Georgian building (No. 9) boasts a magnificent door

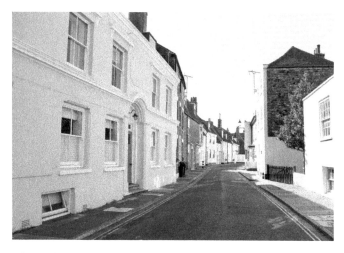 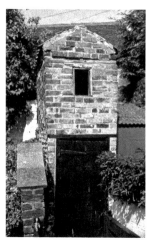

Above left: Redan and a view southward.

Above right: An original herring hangar.

with its impressive fanlight. A blue plaque informs that Sister Edith Appleton, a valiant nurse in the First World War, lived here. Silver Street also boasts splendid Georgian doorways – pediments, pilasters and porticoes – for which this area is renowned.

The Ship is a pleasingly symmetrical early eighteenth-century brick building with its sign of a galleon in glorious sail. The inviting interior retains a nautical flavour with a bar that extends into the snug. The landlord at one time was Captain David Ross RN, who acquired it with his pension. His former shipboard companion, Prince William (later William IV) and also the Duke of Wellington, both visited him here.

Portobello Court, once a place with a dubious reputation, may have been named by a captain who served with Admiral Vernon when he captured Portobello, in Panama, in 1739. Step down to admire the profusion of plants cultivated by today's residents – Deal's mini Kew. The curious neighbouring property was formerly the Blacksmith's Arms.

The lower half of Griffin Street (the Hoop and Griffin stood in Beach Street) has a charming house with a wide bow shop window next to Porthole Cottage. At the top end are the colourful Mary Hougham almshouses displaying a plaque of a trio of heroic lifeboat coxswains.

Dutch Corner is named, naturally, from its spectacular Dutch gables. There are around forty Flemish gables in our conservation area. This particular curvilinear type is actually a Deal gable – a recognised architectural term.

At one time herring hangs (brick sheds where boatmen hung their nets to dry after oiling them) could be found in Exchange Street. This led to the commercial hotel Royal Exchange on the seafront. A cobbled alley (an intriguing survival) runs beside Christmas House at No. 179 Middle Street. Residents of Dolphin Street almost all display dolphin door knockers; in fact, a 'dolphin' is a mooring pole stuck in the water to which boats were tied when they came ashore near here.

North Street leads into spacious Alfred Square presenting public houses at either end: The Prince Albert, with its wide curved double doors, and a community pub, Saracen's Head.

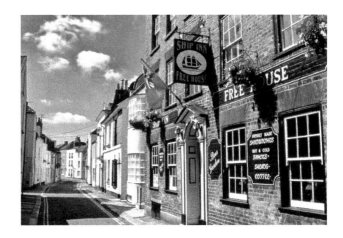

The Ship Inn remains a popular haunt.

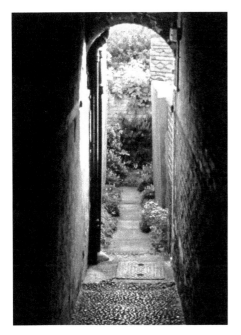

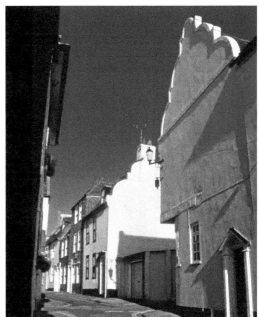

Above left: An intriguing, cobbled alley.

Above right: Dutch Corner with a pair of Deal gables.

DID YOU KNOW?
A conservation area – the first in Kent – was officially designated and is vehemently guarded by the present Deal Society. Deal's renowned conservation area has since been extended several times so that today its abundance of historic properties can be appreciated by townsfolk and visitors alike.

Acknowledgements

With thanks to Councillor Peter Jull and staff at Zoom Photos, Deal, and Marco Orlando for technical advice.

By the Same Author

The Prefab Kid: A Post-war Childhood in East Kent
Wellington at Walmer
Deal: Sad, Smuggling Town
Deal: All in the Downs
Vintage Views of Deal and Walmer
Deal and Walmer: A Celebration, with paintings by Tom Burnham